D0425500

How to Be
a Jewish Grandmother

By Sylvia S. Seaman

HOW TO BE A JEWISH GRANDMOTHER

ALWAYS A WOMAN

MIRACLE FATHER

RUSTY CAROUSEL

How to Be
a Jewish Grandmother

SYLVIA S. SEAMAN

Doubleday & Company, Inc.
Garden City, New York
1979

Excerpts from
HOW TO BE A JEWISH GRANDMOTHER
first appeared in *Modern Maturity*

Drawings by Seymour Chwast

Library of Congress Cataloging in Publication Data

Seaman, Sylvia S
  How to be a Jewish grandmother.

  1. Jews in the United States—Anecdotes,
facetiae, satire, etc.   2. Grandmothers—Anecdotes,
facetiae, satire, etc.   3. Seaman, Sylvia S.
4. United States—Biography—Anecdotes, facetiae,
satire, etc.   I. Title.
E184.J5S397   973'.04'924   [B]
ISBN: 0-385-15205-1
Library of Congress Catalog Card Number 78–22646

Copyright © 1979 by Sylvia S. Seaman

All Rights Reserved
Printed in the United States of America
First Edition

TO

All the grandmothers who don't entirely approve of the way their grandchildren are being brought up.

AND TO

My eight grandchildren—Noah, Elana, Maireda, Shira, Allen, Diana, Colin, and Alida—who made this book possible and who probably won't even like it.

Contents

Introduction:
The Grandmother Mystique

Every female, at some time in her life, is a Jewish grandmother. Some attain this emotional status early, perhaps in adolescence. Others, slower to mature, do not arrive at this stage until they are actually *bubbas.*

It is not even necessary to be a female. Many men may become Jewish grandmothers. It is a state of mind.

Being Jewish is also a state of mind. These days, *everybody* is Jewish. Artists, composers, cabinet members, advisers to Presidents, tailors, actors (regardless of color). A writer these days can't get a book published unless he's depicting the sociological pattern of the Jew in the American scene. If you aren't Jewish, you have to pretend to be.

Grandmothers, in general, fall into one or more of these categories:

Accusers	Analysts	Commanders
Complainers	Forbearers	Guilt-pushers
Martyrs	Naggers	Wailers

You can be a grandmother if you are in any *one* category, but to be a Jewish grandmother, you have to be in at least three, skipping around from one to another so nobody can guess how you'll react.

Anybody, regardless of race, creed, color, or national origin, can be a Jewish grandmother.

Who's Married to Whom—
and Why

Winthrop, my son, the ophthalmologist (that means eye doctor) married to Melanie because her mother said she has to marry a doctor.

Children (all beautiful): Gerald, Arlene, Shira.

Jason, my son, the lawyer, married to Cynthia, the shiksa. Because in every Jewish family one child these days has to marry a Gentile. Children look Gentile, act Jewish. Noah, Colin.

Elana, my daughter, married to Calvin, a college professor. Why? God knows.

Children: Jessica, Jeremy, Sebastian, Gideon. All with fancy names to get away from the Jewish families where every Tom, Dick, and Harry is named David.

Me? I'm married to Harry. Why? We knew why when we got married forty years ago. We still know why—at least twice a week.

How to Be
a Jewish Grandmother

1

Grandmothers Are Unsanitary

When the first grandchild is brought home from the hospital, don't be surprised if the parents won't let you come within twenty feet of the little genius. You aren't allowed to hold him, to bathe him, to feed him, not even to burp him. Admire him, yes—from a distance. Gifts, they permit you to buy. Maybe a few little things like a roomful of nursery furniture or some General Motors stock.

Meanwhile, you'll be seeing a lot of new cameras, exposure meters, tripods, speedlights, projectors. You won't know what each thing is for, but you'll be learning a brand-new vocabulary. You'll be asked to boost the gross national product in the form of washing machines, driers, refrigerators, baby clothing, and toys. Be happy that you are contributing to the nation's prosperity.

About all the wonders of this brilliant baby you will hear, mostly from his father, your son, the doctor.

"When the baby was only one hour and eighteen minutes old," Winthrop tells me, "he had a stepping reflex."

From studying my medical course with Dr. Welby, I didn't find out what's a stepping reflex. My son, a resident in ophthalmology, knows everything, only not as much as he knew when he was only a sophomore in medical school. That was when I had a cold, he gave me a medical lecture and an aspirin.

"This aspirin," said Harry, my husband, "cost a year's tuition."

"Other babies," my son tells me, so proud, "don't have it till they're eight days old."

Winthrop, very thorough, already tested some kind of reflex you hammer the knee and the baby gives you a little kick; and then he tested some kind of Jewish reflex, Balinsky or Babinsky, and some other reflexes *The Reader's Digest* didn't even hear about yet.

I quickly telephone all the great-grandmothers and the great-aunts to boast about it.

"And the baby is very mature," my daughter-in-law Melanie (a doctor's wife knows things, too). "He got his whole fist in his mouth."

"Really?" I gasp.

But I didn't have to worry. It wasn't long before I was also granted the honor of baby-sitting, feeding, bathing, dressing, taking him to the park, sleeping him at my house, cleaning up messy food and bowel movements. Very soon, you find that grandmothers are not as unsanitary as the parents had thought. After a few weeks of getting up nights and debating "Shall we do this, shall we do that?" both parents give up. This week a grandmother, next week the scrubwoman.

To show I'm not an ignoramus, the first time they gave me this great honor to diaper him, I asked, "Do you use the oblong method or the triangle?" In my day it was a catastrophe you should use the wrong method.

"We use the kite method," says Winthrop. He drew me a diagram. He explained. I listened. As soon as they left the house I mislaid the diagram. Who could follow it, anyhow?

When the new mother places your firstborn grand-child on your newly upholstered couch, don't say anything. At least not to the parents. To your friend Frieda Eisenstein, you can say, "They probably think your grandchild's specimen adds a decorator's touch of yellow. In fact, it's a *mitzvah*."

3

When a collage of diapers, infant seat, folding crib, stroller, and bottles are strewn all over your apartment, think of it as "pop" art. Culture!

So your daughter-in-law is overheard to remark, "When you're a grandmother, you shouldn't have beige wall-to-wall carpeting."

So when should you have it?

So now I'm a real grandmother, they need me sometimes, they give me plenty of privileges. When I remember, I keep my mouth shut and my purse open. But mistakes, I'm bound to make.

One day I telephoned. Winthrop answered.

"How's the baby?" I ask, like any grandmother.

"Don't call him the baby," Winthrop scolds. "Call him by his name, Gerald. Otherwise he'll lose his identity."

Winthrop thinks maybe I don't know which baby I'm asking about, or maybe he doesn't know which is which baby.

2

If There's Something You Want to Do—Just Don't

Some things in life are very hard to explain. Like how a girl who wasn't good enough for your son can produce such marvelous grandchildren.

Collect all the funny stories about little Gerald to show how brilliant he is. Tell them often, even if people turn up the TV after the third recital. Tell how your grandson says proudly, "I have a penis, my daddy has a penis, Uncle Moe has a penis." Then he asks you, "Grandma, have you got a penis there?" You do not explain, "Not at the moment."

You also do not explain that when his father was

three years old, he wasn't as smart; he called it his no-no, because every time he touched it, someone said, "No-no." It looked like a small chicken neck with a mushroom on top. What it looks like when it isn't circumcised, I couldn't say. Believe it or not, I never saw one. Never had the pleasure. Now they call things by names my own mother wouldn't have known which parts of the body they were.

When other grandparents tell amusing stories, pretend to listen. Remember, this is give and take. One hand washes the other.

When your grandchild wishes to say something, demand absolute silence from everybody in the room. He may be about to utter a historic statement. When someone else's grandchild interrupts in an ill-mannered way and claims attention, try not to explain that he should be taught some manners.

Do not express yourself freely. Be polite and get ulcers.

Don't explain how good it feels when the grandchildren, having been left at your house for two days, finally go home.

So your husband is a little crude, and what men aren't? He says, "I like to see their little faces come in and I just love to see their little behinds go out."

Emphasize the fact that the grandchildren are adorable now. Do not say to the parents, "Wait till they grow up. Then you'll find out. I only hope they treat you the way you're treating me. I should live to see the day." At least try not to say it, even if you're bursting.

Always carry snapshots of your grandchildren and show them at the slightest provocation. When other people show pictures, don't say, "My grandchildren are better-looking." It's obvious.

If you have color slides or movies of the little sugar-plums, invite people for dinner, but do not warn them. Show little Arlene walking *down* the stairs, little Arlene walking *up* the stairs. Remind yourself that God must love stairs to have given Arlene so many of them.

Do not worry if you overhear a nephew remark, "For one lousy dinner, look what we have to sit and look at."

3

How to Bring Up Your Grandchildren

Tell your daughter:

(a) "Never mind what the doctor says. Who uses a pacifier? Even your grandmother knew better. Why be so low class?"

(b) "Children should be toilet-trained early. What's this *mishugas* that later he'll have to go to a psychiatrist?"

(c) "You shouldn't use a walker. What's the hurry he should walk and get into everything?"

Tell your daughter-in-law:

(a) That you never had such behavior from *your* children.

(b) That your children never ate dessert *before* dinner.

(c) That your children never had hot dogs, olives, or beer.

(d) That you used fresh vegetables, not that frozen stuff and some of those TV dinners.

(e) "Such manners I suppose they learn in that private school. You have to pay good money for it yet. And at two years old you have to get rid of a child in nursery school? Soon," you add with a glow of prophecy, "the teaching will start prenatal."

(f) That *your* children weren't allowed to spend hours every day watching TV like zombies. Never mind explaining that they didn't have television when your children were young. Then it was radio that was going to ruin their lives. Also movies and the music from a Victrola, called canned, like Campbell's soups.

Secretly, now, you wish you'd had television. Such a nice way to keep them Quiet.

When you're doing the baby-sitting, it's different. Let them get educated. Let them learn about smells. The kitchen, the bathroom should be like violets or gardenias. And sweat from the body. Even from the best families. Let them learn that everybody stinks to high heaven. Clothes look clean but smell like pigsties, women sniff around kitchens, bathrooms stink. Husbands blame wives, wives smell husbands' armpits and

9

give them advice. A world like an outhouse. All over America—East, West, North, South—two hundred million people are shooting out from their mouths bad breath. No wonder we have air pollution.

Women got to spray themselves, here, there, you know where, they should be dry. They better watch out for certain places they shouldn't get *too* dry.

And believe me, there are some things that *should* smell.

And hair, on television it bounces, it's so happy. But that's not the way the girls wear it. It used to be, a girl had a date, she curled her hair. Now, it's long and stringy, and my fifteen-year-old granddaughter gets a telephone call from a boy, what does she do?

"I guess you'll want me or your mother to iron your hair."

"Oh, Grandmother," says Arlene, "you're so old-fashioned. Nobody irons hair anymore."

Old-fashioned to me would be rag curlers. Now it's a blow job. I don't mean what you think. It's an electric thing to dry it. The hair, I mean.

All these baseball players showing the kids the boxes of cereals they should eat to be strong. Who needs it? The children should be *more* rambunctious? A cereal they should invent that *takes away* the energy.

Sometimes, it's not so restful. Once, a big fight between Jeremy and Sebastian over what program to watch. Pushing, pulling, punching, me yelling and turning off the TV altogether. And the words they used. Short words boys knew but girls never even heard when I was young. They use those words when they're not angry, just as though it's good, refined English.

Sometimes it's hard to be a modern grandmother. You have to listen to your darlings say words like *luck*—spelled with an f—or maybe *shirt* without the r. Once I heard Jeremy call someone some kind of a sucker. And it wasn't lollipops either, what we used to call an all-day sucker.

When I turned off the TV, Sebastian said, "Grandma doesn't care what happens in the Rose Bowl or the Orange Bowl or the Sugar Bowl. All she cares about is what we do in the toilet bowl."

From grandchildren, you can learn a lot. Only four children, but it seemed like more. Gave me a screaming headache. I went to the medicine cabinet, took out the bottle of aspirin, but I couldn't open it. One of those childproof caps. I had to ask Sebastian, age eight, to show me how.

You listen, you hear. Seven-year-old asks nine-year-old, "What's that thing they call rape on TV?"

"Oh, that!" Big know-it-all nine-year-old explains. "Means when you get all undressed in front of somebody not your mother or not in the family."

That very morning their mother had fired the maid. That's how I happened to be baby-sitting. Later, everything very quiet, the kids playing "Go Fish" and coloring some clowns. I go back to the living room.

Jeremy was explaining to little Gideon, age four. "No, Gideon, you can't fire a grandma."

But from TV they should learn about medicine—high blood pressure, high tension, high cholesterol. It used to be only holidays were high, or someone who drank too much. Now it's hi-fi, hie-lie, high colonic, Hi, Grandma.

About acid indigestion, too—they can see the pills going into the stomach and bubbling around. And sinus. They can see how the body is built, while the little tunnels open up and let the air in.

TV can be as good as Medicare for reducing doctor bills. One day Jessica, age six, telephoned me. "Grandma"—her voice was heartbreaking—"I have a terrible headache. I think it's a brain tumor."

That afternoon I couldn't rush over as I had a luncheon appointment with my friend Frieda, so I say, very soothing, "Must be something you ate." Then I said scientific-like, "Maybe an allergy."

"Would you come over, Grandma?"

"Not right now, honey," I answer, "but if it's a brain tumor, Dr. Welby will cure it."

She felt much better.

Let them watch all the medical shows. This will encourage the little grandsons to grow up to be doctors,
and then with the M.D. license plate they'll be able to
double-park their cars without getting tickets.

4

Grandma Is a Lush

"What is a lush?"

Jessica had been listening halfheartedly to some television travelogue about "the lush green fields of Ireland."

The rest of us, a roomful of visitors, hadn't been listening as Harry, my husband, gives the wrong answer. And how wrong, you'll see.

"That's someone who drinks too much, like whiskey or martinis."

"Oh"—her seven-year-old face lights up—"you mean like Grandma?"

Three children were staying at my house for a long holiday weekend. Their parents were off to Bermuda.

And this conversation was taking place in *my* house, with company yet.

My friend Frieda spoke up. "Which grandma, darling?" All of a sudden Frieda gets so peppy.

Jeremy, Sebastian, and Jessica, sometimes you couldn't get their attention or an answer if you beat a tom-tom, now all three, very lively.

"*This* grandma."

"At that big party."

"You should have seen her. Oh boy!"

Every face in that room, except mine, got ten years younger. Mine, versa visa.

For over a year now, those children never stopped talking about it. My daughter gave a big cocktail party for a friend who wrote a book. Lots of people—editors, critics, people they want to show off for. I take one drink, and I notice *other* people get friendly to me. I take a second drink, and all the company gets very lovable. A third drink, I'm not used to. So I went to lie down in the last bedroom, it's a big apartment, and I closed my eyes.

All of a sudden this bedroom becomes so popular, it's a traffic jam. They should have red and green lights. Women come in to get something from a coat pocket they left on the bed. Others came to unfasten things, to adjust girdles, to loosen straps.

"Look who passed out!" I hear.

Someone needs a mirror (only *this* mirror in this room will do) to powder her face.

"Some people can't resist free liquor."

In the apartment are three bathrooms. But everyone seems to prefer the one connected with this bedroom. It's a parade, a carnival.

I just lie there, my eyes closed so I can hear better; my dress, slinky red, fits nicely when I stand up and don't eat too much, but lying down on the bed, it keeps twisting around and hiking up. And my hair—all afternoon before the party in the beauty parlor and now what that pillow was doing to it was nobody's business. Nobody's but mine.

"Who is she?"

"Don't know, but she must be in the publishing business. You know how *they* are."

"Out cold, like a light."

"And she's no spring chicken, either."

A year ago this happened, and it never happened before or since. And the children, who forget other things, like who gave them the English bicycle for a birthday, never stop mentioning it.

Now they're explaining everything to my guests. Harry . . . is he embarrassed? No. Is he sympathetic? No. Amused he is. Very funny.

"It was only because I didn't remember to eat something with the martinis. Otherwise, I would have been all right," I explain.

"I guess," Jessica says, "there wasn't any food there she didn't like."

"You mean"—someone corrects her—"food she did like."

"No, Grandma only eats food she *doesn't* like."

"Really?" Never before I had such attentive guests.

"Yes, I heard her at the party. A lady said to her, 'How do you keep so slim?' and Grandma said, 'Oh, it's easy. I haven't eaten a thing I like for forty years.'"

This got the first decent laugh for the evening. As you get older, you have to eat less and less every year to keep the same weight, size twelve. Then, one day you decide to go on a binge for your birthday or Mother's Day or something. And what happens? You haven't the old appetite, you can't eat much. The chocolate cake and the butterscotch ice cream just sit there, as far as you're concerned, like a still-life painting. This is some kind of middle-age disaster, some kind of impotence, but not the worst kind.

Then Jeremy, no one should get ahead of him, adds his two cents. "At the beginning of the party, Grandma looked nice. She had on a long dress. When Daddy introduced her to some dame, he said, 'Meet my mother,' and the dame said, 'Gee, I wish I had a mother who looked like that.' But, oh boy, oh boy, you shoulda seen Grandma later. All messed up. And her hair, gee!"

Next time the parents dash off for Bermuda they can take the children with them.

And leave them there.

5

God Bless Grandma

You have given your beautiful granddaughter Jessica a gorgeous dress. Just the right color for her red-gold hair, just the right size for her now, not to grow into. She looked adorable in it when she tried it on.

Then you wait to see her wear it. You wait one week, two weeks, a month, two months. Not a sign of it. You sneak a look in the closet. Yes, it's there. They haven't given it to the maid. Not yet.

So do not say anything to Jessica. But one day, when both parents are present, ask casually, "Where is that handmade, hand-embroidered French voile dress that I brought from that *boutique* on the Rue de la Paix in Paris?"

"Oh, we're saving it for a special occasion. It's too good to wear just any time."

So do not mention all the special occasions—the birthday parties, the various gatherings of the *mishpucha*—on which the dress did not appear. Above all, do not mention the aunts, great-aunts, and cousins who would have gotten nervous breakdowns from the competition if they'd seen the dress.

At these parties, always there's several of the same kind of presents—piggy banks, pictures of sailing ships, transistor radios, blankets. This way you know which relatives opened new accounts in which banks.

The little apron flaunting across the bib, "I Love Grandma," you yourself can put on Jessica when you visit. If it is no longer hanging in the closet, you'll find it among the dust rags. Gerald's sweatshirt, boasting "Grandma loves me, God bless her," is nowhere to be found.

But, if without your having mentioned it again, Jessica suddenly is wearing the Parisian dress, it's a very bad sign. It means they are going to ask you for a very special favor, involving time, effort, and probably money.

1. They want you to keep four children over the three-day Fourth of July weekend so they can go to Grossinger's. You aren't going away, anyhow.

Or 2. Jessica, age four and so musical, needs a Steinway baby grand piano. They want the two hundred and odd dollars you have in her bank account; they'll add some and you can add what you intend to give her for birthdays, *Chanukah*, Halloween, Columbus Day, Lincoln's Birthday, Flag Day, and other occasions during the next ten years, including the gift of money you will undoubtedly give her when she goes away to college.

At this point, take a stand.

"I will not, positively not," you say, "include her wedding present. For this we'll wait till she gets married. That is," I add, "if it's still classy enough to get married. Nowadays"—I show I'm a sociologist like everybody else—"it's only fashionable for priests and nuns to marry."

Be firm! You have only about twenty years, give or take a few, before you have to decide on the exact amount. Besides, how do you know now what the other side of the family will be giving?

But there's one present I gave I don't have to follow up on. Ten dollars to Jeremy for his birthday. He went to Zum Zum and ordered every dessert on the bulletin board. "I had apple strudel, strawberry sundae with whipped cream, marble cake, cocoanut pie, chocolate mint sundae—two of them, cherry strudel, jelly doughnuts," he says.

"How do you feel?" I was worried.

"Wonderful, Grandma. Just wonderful."

"I'm glad you enjoyed yourself."

"You know what? It was the best day of my whole life." Jeremy, age fourteen.

And you know what? If he lives to be ninety-five, it could still turn out it was the best day of his life.

6

A Cat House
Is a House for Cats

My grandmother used to keep cats in the house because the lady mice didn't take birth-control pills. My grandchildren keep cats just for hugging and kissing. When I come to visit they hold the cats up to my face, I gotta kiss them, too. I'll kiss them, but I don't have to love them. These days, like everybody else, I can be full of identity.

Winthrop's children, Gerald, Arlene, and Shira, each has a private cat: Supercat, Copycat, and Louise. Every week or so one of them has to be rushed to the vet—his fur is unhealthy-looking, he isn't eating his Little Friskies, or he had a fight with one of the other cats and his ear is bleeding. With the life those cats lead, I don't know what they have to fight about. With the vet they should fight. For fifty dollars he takes away sex so the girl cat shouldn't have to worry about rape.

A good vet makes more than a pediatrician, and no house calls.

Dr. Spock won't let you beg your children to eat. Bad for their psyches. But cats, you can tempt, you can beg with the kind of food he won't walk away from. They're better fed than the kids because they don't get any junk food—Cokes, frankfurters, candy, potato chips —things with all the calories emptied out.

Without a cat on the lap, the children couldn't watch TV, all the time brushing the fur with a special cat brush. The cat has to watch TV, too, to find out what's the most expensive canned food he can eat.

So when there was a big cat show at the Hotel McAlpin, I offered to take Shira. An hour before I was to pick her up, she phoned.

"Is it O.K. if I bring a friend?"

"Of course, darling."

They never step foot out of the house without at least one friend.

The girls wore jeans, ragged at the bottom. They keep cutting them they shouldn't be too even. And dirty is better, too. If they don't look faded enough, they dip them in Clorox. A hole at the knee is the classiest.

Long, straight hair covered half their faces. Even if I could have seen the other half of the girl friend's face, I wouldn't have known if it was Pam or Alison or Linda or which Pam or which Alison or which Linda. Once, one of the granddaughters brought home a new friend. I knew it couldn't last—a girl with the old-fashioned name of Agnes.

The blouses they wore looked like the colors ran in the wash. And lots of beads and seashells hanging. Every day they look ready for trick or treat.

So to the Hotel McAlpin, but first, lunch at Mary Elizabeth's, then a new scarf at Altman's (it was on the way), and then to the hotel's first floor, the cat house. Not the kind of cat house I used to hear about.

Each cat was in a cage alone. Believe me, the cats didn't seem to be having much fun. Lots of spraying with smelly powder was going on.

Also, lots of brushing. More brushing than most kids' hair gets in a month. No wonder the cats' fur looks better.

Hundreds of cages, all sizes, all colors, some with fancy names on the cages. Shira had to be personally introduced to dozens of them. Full of questions, full of admiration. The owners adored Shira. I was getting to a state of exhaustion where I wasn't adoring Shira.

I heard Shira explaining how her Persian cat, Louise, with the long silky gray-and-white fur had a long, high-class pedigree. No wonder, I thought, that cat walks around so hoity-toity and acts like even if he could, he wouldn't talk to me. Persian? Yeah, yeah. Must be a Litvak.

Then came an announcement over the loudspeaker: "Have your cat immortalized in the lobby." This means they take his picture. Life-size if you love him enough.

At this point, I was wishing immortalizing meant they stuffed him.

When we left the show, I said, "Where shall we go for ice cream?" After all, you can't let children starve. It was already an hour and a half since they had chocolate pie with whipped cream—survival rations. Meaning that they are able to survive until the next meal. With such disasters, you can't take a chance. Their stomachs might shrink.

My eight-year-old Shira was quick with the answer, "Let's go to a topless restaurant."

Me! Deadpan. The muscles on my face—frozen like it just came out of the ice-cube tray. I didn't bat an eyelash. You do too much batting with a false eyelash, it's liable to drop off.

"It's so cold." I suggested: "Let's go home and have hot chocolate and cherry pie."

"All right, Grandma. Anyway I think it'd be too cold

to have ice cream in a topless restaurant—the kind without a roof."

"Besides," says Pam-Alison-Linda, "the cats may be getting lonely for us."

So home we went to Supercat, Copycat, and Louise.

7

On Baby-sitting

If you meet anyone who tells you that she baby-sits with her grandchildren every weekend, that she takes her little darlings to the playground, enjoys every minute of it, and lets the parents go out Saturday nights, you must not mention this to your daughter-in-law or even to your daughter.

To your friend Frieda, you can say, "You know what Fanny said? That she baby-sits every weekend. You believe it?"

"No, not a word. Besides, if it's true, it won't last long. It's only her first grandchild."

To Frieda, you can tell anything as long as it's not

something bad about yourself. With her, it goes in one ear and out the telephone.

However, if you meet another grandmother who explains: "I *never* baby-sit. Why should I? I didn't do it for my own children when I could get out of it, I won't do it for my grandchildren."

Quote her lengthily, and often.

If your children hire a baby-sitter, warn them not to trust her.

"Who knows what she'll do to those wonderful darlings!"

Jealousy, natural jealousy, is there between mother-in-law and daughter-in-law. When it's time to baby-sit, this doesn't show. She needs you, and though you won't admit it to her, you need her. You're really dying to be alone with the grandchildren. Then you can hug them and kiss them till you're blue in the face. In front of the parents you dassent be too snuggly. If they see the children love you too much—a granddaughter asked to have a thumb kissed, she just remembered she hurt it a week ago last Tuesday—parents can get a little snippy. About something else, of course. But if it's an errand, to go to the kitchen for chocolate milk or to wipe a runny nose, this kind of love is O.K.

If a parent is yelling at a child, never take the child's part, except maybe later when the parent isn't there.

Besides, nowadays the children don't need so much protection. Once when Melanie, my daughter-in-law, was shouting, Shira spoke up.

"Mother, don't scream at us. We children have our rights, too."

When you go to baby-sit, whether it's your daughter's house or your daughter-in-law's, show character. Don't move things. Don't take the floor lamp from the spot near the couch and put it next to a chair. Maybe just change one small vase from one table to another. Don't rearrange the chairs for more convenient seating, even if it brings on an attack of indigestion.

Look in the refrigerator, be refined, don't say anything, just have no expression on your face when you look at the leftovers they are going to leave for your supper while they go to a fancy restaurant. "Recycled food," your son calls it. Take the pot roast cooking on the stove and add several items like bay leaves and paprika. Always explain the reason.

"The children like it better my way."

Don't explain that what the children like best is real American food like pizza and chicken chow mein.

After the children are asleep is the time to look through the drawers and closets. You find there are twice as many wire hangers in the hall closet as there were last time. Where do they all come from and don't they throw any away? What goes on between the hangers in the dark closet after the door is closed? Whatever it is, those hangers aren't using contraceptives.

When you let them dump the children on you for an afternoon or overnight, remember that parents these days are not like we were with our schedules and diets and rules that drove everybody crazy. But don't haul out the infant at midnight to show him off to your guests. You have a collapsible crib and playpen combination at your home. What this country needs is a collapsible grandmother.

Dr. Spock, God bless him, says parents are only human. Grandparents, too. This means that when you can't stand it anymore, it's O.K. to give the child a good whack. Dr. Benjamin Spock won't object.

You can keep the children at your house for a week before anybody'd phone and ask where and how and what. You can keep them until they're ready to be sent off to college.

Finally, you decide to take them back to their home. On the telephone, your daughter says, "All right. Bring the children home but not the puppy. Keep him until next week."

Be careful you don't put your daughter in a panic or

hysteria. Just deliver the grandchildren to her *before* dinner, and you'll see a classic case of nervous breakdown.

Don't be surprised when you come one day to help out with the sewing, the baby-sitting, the reading, the diapering, little Jessica, now a mature six-year-old, says, "We don't need you today, Grandma. We have a maid."

So you go in the kitchen to have a look what's going on. A nice-looking colored girl is peeling potatoes. You are careful-like, you don't say, "No one peels potatoes anymore, you take away all the minerals under the skin, you cook in jackets."

The maid, colored a nice copper like the bracelet my friend Frieda wears for arthritis, used to be called *Negro*. Now it's an insult. You gotta say *black*.

But in Jewish, it was always *black*. The girl that came on Thursdays to do the cleaning was *die Schvartze*. In English that means *the black*.

Once I heard the maid answer the phone. Someone at the other end must have asked who was talking. So I heard the answer "I'm the Schvartze."

We Jews were always ahead of our time.

8

The Free-enterprising Grandmother

When the Other Grandmother brings Colin a box of tin automobiles for his birthday, be cultured. Don't say, "Is that all you're giving your grandchild?" Give her a look. Show you're trying to hide your opinion.

She will say, "This isn't *all* I'm giving. I put twenty-five dollars in his bank account."

Naturally, you do not believe a word of it. Except now she'll have to do it.

But just to be on the safe side, you will give Colin a check for thirty-five dollars. This must be done at the table, just after the candles are blown out and when all the adults are standing behind the youngsters' chairs, wondering how soon they'll get coffee and cake themselves.

Fold the check so nobody can read it. Money is so crass. But don't worry, the child's mother will open it, announce the amount, and squeal with delight. That fixes the Other Grandmother.

When the party is for your son or daughter, let them know that candles on the cake are only for children.

"Not dignified for grown-ups," you say.

The reason for this you do not explain, but this is what happened on my son Jason's last birthday party.

Colin asked, "Grandma, how come Daddy is forty-three and you're only thirty-nine?"

"I married very young."

Everyone around the table laughs, nasty-type sounds, and Colin, age six, has a funny expression on his face.

"You mean, Grandma, you were only four years old when Daddy was born?"

Next year he goes into second grade. His arithmetic will get better. Mine, God willing, won't.

Some of the older children who, worse luck, somehow found out my real age, just love to mention it, especially when there's company. The way those kids mention my age would be O.K. only if they were talking about brandy.

You shouldn't always give the most expensive presents to the grandchildren from the one that struck it rich. Not always. Sometimes give a rich-looking present to the grandchildren from the ones that didn't do so well.

And politeness should be democratic, too. You shouldn't always be more polite to the ones that have more money. Just because they have a Park Avenue apartment doesn't mean you can't tell them off once in a while. But in a refined way. And don't be afraid of the sleep-in maid.

The grandchildren, like children of divorced parents, learn to play off one grandmother against the other.

"Grandma Becky always takes us in a taxi."

You can take them for a ride in a horse and carriage through Central Park for only fifteen dollars for the first half hour. Some bargain.

Show the Other Grandma how intellectual you are. Take them to the Planetarium and the Hall of Science. Never mind if they start to fidget. One of them, thank God, will love it, like the time Jeremy came home and told his father, "We saw the whole world and the Empire State Building."

When they boast that the Other Grandmother took them to Longchamps for lunch, don't let the grass grow under your feet. Promptly take them to the Plaza. When you come out, Arlene will undoubtedly say, "I wish Daddy would take us to McDonald's again. It was fun eating hamburgers from a box."

Of course, after hearing that they were taken to the movies, not around the corner, but to Radio City, you have to take them to a Broadway musical.

I love the movies, especially the sad ones. You see other people's troubles, they're terrible. You see a woman—she's a widow, or she's divorced, she's lonely as all get out. Like all single women, she's afraid to say "No" to any invitation. You come home, you have a big fight with your husband. It's a pleasure!

At the Broadway musical, the children get fidgety, much they can't understand, and it takes too long before they can go to the rest room or get their ice cream.

After the performance, Jessica will ask, "Grandma, when are you going to take us to see Mary Poppins again? Jeremy saw it five times and I only saw it four times."

9

The Creamed-chicken Grandmothers

How much creamed chicken can a person eat in a life-time? No end to ladies luncheons. And all for worthy causes. Your stomach may be a worthy cause, too, but you must think first of Biafra—creamed chicken. For Bangladesh—creamed chicken. For Ethiopia, for Mozambique, for Angola. Something happens in Africa—a revolution, not enough rain—and all these grandmothers have to eat creamed chicken at one o'clock in New York.

Years ago you ate for Spain—for the loyal ones—for orphans in Korea, for Indians, not the ones with feathers, the ones with saris.

The chicken comes with some kind of gooey sauce we used to call library paste. Always some green peas on the side. Someone always complains and turns up her Jewish nose. (What she wouldn't give to have it turned up permanently!)

"You eat for Israel," someone says, "you'd think they'd give you at least some *flanken*."

Someone's always selling you a ticket. The mucilage they use to hold the chicken from falling off the plate also holds people together. That's why it's not hard to sell your book of tickets and the raffle tickets, too. The lunch gives everyone a chance to catch up on important events, like whose daughter had an abortion, whose grandson didn't get admitted to Yale.

"His marks were too high," his grandmother explained.

"How come?"

"They had to take a Negro with low marks."

"The quota system. It used to be for Jews."

Meanwhile, you look around to see what everybody's wearing. And what's nifty. A new mink stole.

"She had it made over from her daughter's old mink coat."

"That blue beaded dress she's wearing. Believe me, it doesn't owe her anything."

One woman, Mrs. Applebaum, everything she wears has to be a Pucci or a Gucci. Hoochie-coochie was a dance I did when a girl. No connection.

"See over there, Sadie. That dress with the green Bertha collar. She must have had that hanging in her closet for years already."

"She should have left it there. It wasn't asking to be fed."

You see two ladies talking, very serious, very excited, you can't hear what they're saying, but you can tell, right off, that *someone, someplace,* has a hell of a nerve.

One luncheon, at the Hilton, we all agreed in whispers, "Don't ask Julia about her daughter's divorce. She's too upset about it."

Everybody was tactful. No mention of it. Finally comes dessert.

"Oh, mushmelon."

"Nobody calls it mushmelon for forty years. Called cantaloupe."

"You live long enough you talk a language your grandchildren don't understand. They think it's like Shakespeare."

Finally, Julia couldn't stand it anymore. To me, sitting next to her, she says, "Funny, nobody asks about my daughter."

"So, how is she taking it?"

Julia closes her eyes, breathes deep like a doctor has a stethoscope on her chest, and sighs, "Don't ask."

Sometimes, instead of eating for causes, you get to eat

for pleasure. Frieda's husband hasn't been retired very long, she gets nervous, not used to it yet. Her children live in *goyishe* places like Arizona or Montana—you fly there for a visit you have to bring a whole pastrami and kosher salami—so she's always on the telephone with ideas to get her out of the house. So she digs up fancy restaurants where the waiter flips open the napkin and puts it, personally, over your crotch.

"You know, I hear you're nobody"—she laughs to show it's a joke—"but nobody, if you haven't eaten at Pearl's."

"Who's Pearl? Never was invited to anyone's house named Pearl."

"It's a Chinese restaurant."

So we go to Pearl's downtown and we have the same egg foo young and chicken chop suey we could eat on Broadway, only it costs three times as much because you have to phone first to reserve a table.

The next week it turns out you're nobody, just nobody, if you haven't thrown out your money at Elaine's.

Next, Maxwell Plums. Just an expensive omelette, or you're nobody.

And you know what?

I'm still nobody.

10

Be a Psychologist

If your daughter, Elana, quotes Spock to prove she's right about what she's doing, give different advice from Gesell.

If she quotes Gesell, hold on to Spock.

Remind her, not often, but every once in a while, how she taught the children to call their parents by their first names "to destroy the barriers to communication." And how, after a few days in kindergarten, her darling Jessica came out of school very depressed. I was the one who called for her that day.

"What's the matter, dear?" I asked.

"Why don't I have a mommy and daddy like other kids? Didn't I come out of anyone's stomach?"

With children, they ask questions, always you got to be honest and give them the facts even if you have to make them up.

Now she's interested where babies come from. How soon, I wonder about this generation, she'll be interested in how to stop them from coming? Her mother will tell her, early yet.

My daughter, Elana, reads all the psychology books. When little Jeremy takes a hammer and smashes your compact, you're not supposed to open your mouth. That day Elana read someplace, "He's going through his Aggressive Phase."

Believe me, I only wished it was her day for reading a different book.

When she butters little Sebastian's bread, warn her about cholesterol.

When she serves Jessica Coca-Cola, remind her of the caffeine in it.

If she offers the children spinach, speak scientifically: "The iron they used to think was in spinach, isn't."

Your daughter may plead fatigue and skip the children's bath. You must speak up, for her own good.

"That's one thing I never did when you were little." How can she remember, anyhow?

Stick to your roles of dietitian, doctor, and psychologist.

You will see your poor, mistreated grandchildren drinking soda; warn their parents about their teeth and the sugar in it.

If they are given, the innocent, unsuspecting lambs, a sugar-free soda, sigh heavily.

"The side effects of the sweetener they use may be harmful. Nothing proved yet."

For *my* mother, a green vegetable was a sour pickle. Me, I'm more advanced. Spinach by the ton I shoveled down my children's throats. But everything changes.

"I'm just waiting," I tell my daughter, "for the day some diet man comes out, he just *proved* spinach is *bad* for you. Stuffs up the kidneys, sits on your gall bladder or something."

If the little darlings are eating well (at *your* house, where else?) and you say something tactful like, "When the food is good, see how nicely they eat," don't get upset when your daughter-in-law says, "Don't encourage obesity. If they store up fat cells, it persists into adulthood."

The trouble nowadays is that children eat everything —but everything. You can't give them anything to spoil their appetites; they already had Good Humors, pickles and Yoo-Hoo. But if you give them ice cream and cake before you deposit them at their home for dinner, you can be sure they won't eat for your daughter-in-law.

You confide in the Other Grandma. "Those children may *look* healthy, but they're really undernourished."

About psychology, my children and their spouses know a lot.

"No one"—they educate me—"should hesitate to show hostility toward a parent."

What they don't tell me, maybe I need a little more education, is that a mother-in-law, if she knows which side her bread is buttered on, should never show hostility to a daughter-in-law. This is a special relation and should have a name like that thing between mother and son, called Oedipus. This is when a mother and a good son have a natural affection for each other. This is very dangerous. Both must have psychiatric help for years.

To my two daughters-in-law, I have no special hard feelings. Only sometimes, like toward everyone else you love, or don't. If things have a special name, they're easier to handle. You read about it, hear about it, know that everybody has the same trouble, and you don't worry so much about your mean feelings. But toward the psychologists, believe me, I got plenty hostility.

Even the grandchildren become psychologists. So much they know, they ought to have diplomas hanging on the walls. One evening, Noah was sleeping at my house. Suddenly, from the bedroom, comes cries, loud.

I rushed in, hugged him, and asked, "What's the matter, darling?"

"I had a bad dream," he sobbed.

I stroked his golden hair. Six years old in October, our Noah. Named for that circus man in the Bible, the one who was drunk all the time. He wasn't a Jew either. No wonder they have the song "*Shiker* Is a *goy.*"*

"Tell Grandma all about it, dear."

He sat up, straight, stopped crying, and said, "No. This isn't something you tell your grandmother. I'll only tell it to an analyst. And what's more"—his voice getting stronger every minute—"I want my own analyst, like everybody else has."

* The Drunkard Is a Gentile.

11

How to Encourage Art and Culture

To be a good grandmother you have to learn lots of "don'ts." It's something like your childhood, when every sentence from a grown-up started with "Don't."

If your grandson is taking guitar lessons, don't say, "Whoever heard of a child playing a guitar? Segovia, he won't be."

Maybe the grandson in high school seems to like only football, watches every game on TV, talks only football. Plays after school. Is this a business for a Jewish boy?

"Take away the football," tell his mother, "and get

him a violin." If Gerald plays the violin like his musical Uncle Moe, who didn't keep it up, applaud, but don't say, "Another Mischa Elman." Besides, they won't know who Mischa Elman was anyhow. Only from the Beatles they know.

When your grandchild, in a hushed atmosphere, recites a poem, don't say, "Another John Barrymore."

If your granddaughter dances, don't say, "Another Pavlova." Everybody can see for themselves. You mention the name of a star, it only dates you, anyhow.

Don't make comparisons with other people's grandchildren; just smile.

Be restrained, be polite, don't be vulgar. Don't explain that you are paying for the lessons. There are other ways you can see to it they'll find out.

Don't make one grandchild a favorite. Don't buy him the best toys. Don't take him frequently to puppet shows, the Children's Zoo, and museums. Don't develop a secret vocabulary and secret jokes with him. Don't make comparisons with the other children. The little sweetie-pie, whom you are smothering with love and gifts, and no one is supposed to know it, will love it and brag about it. But according to the most recent psychiatric research, he should feel that if he requires so much special attention, he must be an imbecile.

Most of the time, just don't.

12
Grandma's Childhood Is a Fairy Tale

A grandparent was never a baby. Grandparents were never young, never in love, never lived the days of wine and roses. How could they? They're so old, so different from people.

But the grandchildren just love to hear fairy tales. And one of their favorites is the ridiculous ideas we, the grandparents, used to have. Not that they believe it all, but it's a nice way to spend a rainy afternoon. Their mother is out demonstrating they should let women in one of those saloons they wouldn't go into anyhow if they were allowed, the maid is in the basement a long time with the washing machine and the handyman, the Monopoly games and the Scrabble peter out, and the fights begin.

"Grandma," says Shira, "tell us about some of those silly ideas you used to have."

"Well," I start, "cold baths were good for you. They closed the pores."

"What's pores?" from Colin.

"Like little openings in the skin."

"You have to close them like a door?"

"That's right. You opened them with a hot bath, then closed them with a cold bath."

"Why?"

"God knows! Only," I explain, "anything horrible was *good* for you. Medicine didn't do you any good unless it was nasty, like a long walk before breakfast. When you were dying of hunger and maybe cold too, in winter." Suddenly I remembered. "They used to say 'Early to bed and early to rise, makes a man healthy, wealthy, and wise.'"

"Did it?" asks Shira.

"No. Everybody got up early because they had to go to work." I paused. "From this I never saw any millionaires."

"Did you do those stupid things?" asks Jeremy.

"Not often. Sometimes I tried. The rest of the time I just felt guilty. My mother nagged me. Said I wasn't healthy."

"Were you?"

"Sure. I was healthy but I didn't look it. I was skinny. So all the aunts and uncles said I'd never get a husband."

"Did you?" asks Colin.

"Who do you think Grandpa Harry is?"

"Oh! I didn't know. He's so old to get married to."

"When you went to the country, maybe a farm in the Catskills, you went to get fat. Your mother and your grandmother stuffed you with cheese blintzes with sour cream and potato latkes. And they wouldn't let you do much exercise, afraid you'd run it off. 'Just sit,' they'd say."

"Did you get fat?"

"No. But by the time I was ready to marry, times changed, you were supposed to be thin. Then the aunts nagged me to wear a corset. Said if I didn't, I'd get fat. And you were supposed to wear it as soon as you got up in the morning. Otherwise you were a slob. And you had to get dressed right away. No wrapper."

"What's a wrapper?" asks Shira.

"A housecoat."

"Oh, I thought it was one of those girls that wrapped up the gift boxes."

"No. It covered up the corset."

"Did you?"

"What?"

"Wear a corset?"

"No, never. And I didn't get fat until I was nursing your father."

"Did you stay fat?"

"What am I now?"

"I don't know. Thin, I guess. Were the aunts right? You had a lot of trouble getting a man?"

"Well," I boast, "I had no trouble getting a husband because I could play 'Für Elise' on the piano."

Surprise on their faces. No idea what I was talking about.

"To get a good husband," I explain, "a girl had to have accomplishments. This meant playing the piano. And never popular songs or ragtime. Until you could play a piece called 'Für Elise,' you were nobody, absolutely nobody."

Those faces still without a bit of intelligence.

"Grandma"—Shira's face gets lively—"tell us again how you went to a store where everything costs only five cents or ten cents."

"Woolworth's. Called the five-and-ten."

All the children burst into laughter, rolled on the floor, it was so funny.

"You still call it the five-and-ten, Grandma."

"I know, I forget. So you're laughing," I say. "But when you're grandparents, children will be laughing at the funny things you're doing and saying now."

Jeremy scoffed. "How could they? We aren't doing anything funny." All agreed.

"Tell us," said Shira, "other things bad for you, like you once told us, bananas and Coke."

"Coke," I said, "is still bad for you." The first time I said it they paid no attention. Why now—the twentieth time?

"How can it be?" Full of logic, my darlings. "We have it right in the refrigerator."

I think a while. So many things we like now were verboten. Had to do them on the sly. And I don't mean things like taking dope or masturbating. Believe it or not, you weren't supposed to neck or even kiss until you were engaged. Of course, we did. Some things you didn't even tell your girl friends. Some things you never tell your grandchildren.

Safer topics, you explain. "Naps in the daytime were very bad for you."

"Suppose you were tired."

"Bad for your health. Bad for character."

"Even if you were sick."

"Sick it was O.K. But not to sleep with flowers in the room."

"It was too pretty?" asks Jeremy.

"Took all the oxygen out of the room."

"What's oxygen?"

"Something you breathe."

"Where is it?"

"Can't see it."

"How'd you know it's there?" asks Colin, scientific.

"As far as I'm concerned," I sigh, "you don't."

Now I was running out of things to remember.

"Oh," I said, "very few people, only the very rich, had automobiles."

"Gee, that must have been terrible. You had to take taxis all the time."

"Taxis!" Even I was amazed. "We were lucky if we had a nickel for carfare. Less than thirty blocks, we walked."

Never so much attention to every word I say. No running into the kitchen for soda or Fudgicles or potato chips. No one even had to go to the toilet. Shira didn't have any phone calls to make.

"More! More! More!" shouting.

"Well"—I thought of something—"my grandmother had to hang socks out in the backyard, always in pairs."

"Why?"

"So the neighbors, they shouldn't talk."

This was so silly they weren't even interested.

"You didn't use cosmetics. That was for street-walkers. A little talcum to take off the shine was all right. Only at home, though. Never in public. Wasn't nice to comb your hair, either. And you never ate outdoors, except candy or ice cream. At a picnic, O.K. But on the street, never. No sandwiches, frankfurters, pizza, not even an apple or banana."

"Oh, Grandma. Now you're making things up."

So laughable, they forgot to ask me what's a streetwalker. Other words for it, they'd know.

Well, if I was making things up, I'd try one more true thing they wouldn't believe.

"It wasn't nice to die from cancer."

They stared at me. "It's not nice to die, anyway," says Colin.

"Yeah, but it was worse from cancer. You didn't tell anybody. A heart attack was more refined like."

"Silly."

Then I had a remembrance they won't forget till they're a hundred and twenty years old.

"When I was little, about ten years old, you weren't supposed to go to the movies."

This was the way to get such attention you get only with a five-pound box of Barricini, mostly with cherries in liquor.

"Not go to the movies!" Horror on the faces like they just saw Dracula come out of the bedroom.

"Nope," I say, "it was trash, bad for your character, showed you had no culture, and worse, it was bad for the eyes. Always stories about people going blind right in the movie house."

End talk. Nothing to follow such an act. Besides, who can believe such *bubba meisses* from a crazy grandmother?

13

Grandmothers Are Given Special Privileges

My daughter, Elana, says she's doing me a big favor, giving me a real treat. While she and her husband are taking a vacation in Latin America—Guatemala, Cosa Nostra, and so on—I'll have the privilege of staying with the four grandchildren I adore, she says. Now, I thought, I'll snoop around and find out what they did with that expensive Belgian linen tablecloth and napkins I gave them.

No housework, she says. The maid does everything. No, I'll have nothing to do except the shopping and deciding what to eat and the worrying, did the children wear their boots, it's raining, and where is that grandson, it's so late already and he's not home, and did they take their vitamins, and Jeremy has to be taken to the dentist for adjusting his braces. Jessica's on the telephone the whole evening, did she finish her homework, and tomorrow after school I take her to her ballet lessons, with ice cream and pizza after. The mornings are a special pleasure. Only to wheel the baby over the curbs up, and curbs down, across streets to the park. Cute, he is. A rest cure, he's not.

My literary daughter quotes Margaret Mead. "Grandparents are our greatest unused resources." What does she mean, unused?

All this I'm supposed to do cheerfully. Yeah, yeah, cheerful like the way Macy's refunds money.

I'm there, says Elana, for security. National security? With everything else I have to do, who has time for wiretapping, breaking into psychiatrists' offices, and erasing tapes?

My husband, Harry, says he'll deprive himself of the pleasure. He'll stay home and only visit us for dinner— stuffed peppers, matzoh ball soup, while the children eat hamburgers and franks and drink Cokes.

My husband, Harry, the name I should explain. You know how it is in the beauty parlor window, a sign says, "Pierre is now here. Formerly with Yvette." They mean Pierre, formerly Pete, and Yvette used to be

Yetta. It's the same with Harry. Formerly Hymie. Until my daughter, Elana, started to date. Then the name, Hymie, she said, wasn't ecumenical enough. That means it was too ethnic. Even sounded like the Spanish Jaime.

After dinner he goes to the senior citizens club. This week he's organizing something. Gets a bunch together and starts lecturing:

"We should organize, protest, scream, and hit. We elder statesmen are an abused minority. We don't want to be treated as though we're senile, stupid, just waiting to die."

He gets everyone to sign something they'll send to their congressman. What the congressman will do about it, I don't know. Some won't sign.

"I don't want to be in the secret files of the CIA," they explain.

The day Elana and her husband, Calvin (named after his grandfather, Kalman), left, they had to take a late evening plane because it was Thursday. On Thursdays, my daughter goes to some kind of meeting where men and women raise consciences. What else they raise, only God Old Mighty knows. Meanwhile, the kids at home raised hell.

One big fight they had, Jessica called her brothers "male chauvinist pigs." "All men are like that," she tells me.

"Even Grandpa Harry?" I ask, knowing how she adores him.

"Oh, he's just a plain male chauvinist." Grandfathers are still way up on top, getting respect.

Chauvinist, he is. When I ring an elevator bell, he has to push the button, too. Thinks the elevator is male and only comes for men. In the elevator he can hardly wait to get upstairs to pee. He dances around, first on one foot, then on the other. Hops, jumps, twirls.

"Such dance steps," I tell him, "you didn't do since the Bunny Hug and the Lindy Hop."

"These," says Harry, "I'm going to have choreographed."

Elevators in my family, new problems. Shira won't ride in one that doesn't have music.

"Too scary when it's quiet," she says. How modern can a child get, I ask you?

Women's libbers, and my daughter, think they, personally, invented orgasms. Believe me, she doesn't know my generation. That's because we didn't shoot our mouths off about everything we did and shouldn't have, and we didn't need public meetings to talk about it. When a man looked at us a certain way, you think we didn't know what was dancing in his head? Visions. But not from sugarplums. Sure, we didn't have open marriage. But that didn't mean we weren't open to suggestions. I'll match my orgasms, then and now, against theirs any time.

Elana and Calvin and the suitcases, each weighed in at forty-four pounds, were ready to leave. So everybody got kissed and hugged and warned and off they went. One thing you can say for today's parents, different from us. Practically no instructions. Full of permissions. Only about the plants, she gave me plenty rules. To the children I can say anything I want, but to the plants I must talk nicely. Show them affection. Don't insult her gentians. The only way I can remember the name of these flowers is by thinking of genitals. *That* word, I can remember.

I wonder if plants are like dogs and get to look like their owners. Well, plants, at least, listen to you, with good manners, and don't talk back. But when you get mad at a plant, who do you talk to? The frozen vegetables? Remind her, I don't, about my black thumb. Even artificial plants in my house seem to dry up. Maybe I should be more polite to my plastic trailing ivy. But talk, I'll try. Maybe it'll turn out I have a green tongue.

For the children, no warnings. In our day we were full of rules. Schedules. Strict. Whatever you did, it shouldn't be easy. If it was convenient, it wasn't good for the baby. Teaching about the toilet started with three months. Now, if a grown-up goes to a psychiatrist the whole problem comes from early toilet training.

Psychiatrists say, "We can always spot a Watson baby." If a baby cried at four minutes to feeding time, the poor thing had to cry the full four minutes before he got his food. The poor babies weren't fed when they were hungry. Now the babies are fed when they're not hungry. Drowned, they are, in milk. Everything on time in the old days. The dot of two, feeding, the dot of seven, bath, dot of nine, potty chair. The more dots the better the mother.

Those days, if you didn't go to college, you didn't know how to raise a child. Nowadays, it's different, thank God. You don't even have to be intelligent. We read Watson, not Mr. Elementary-My-Dear-Watson, another Mr. Watson who invented something he called Behaviorism. That meant that if a child didn't behave right and sassed you back, you shouldn't give him a smack. What you should do, I can't remember, but whatever it was, it didn't work any better than whatever it is they do now. There's still a lot of noisy pushing and shoving and kicking and sibling rivalry. You weren't supposed to spoil the baby. If you never hugged and kissed him, he'd grow up to win the Nobel Prize. Every time you gave the baby a little cuddle, on the sly, mind you, you felt like a criminal. Everybody went around feeling guilty about all sorts of things. Usually about the wrong things, too. (Just like now.)

All kinds of child-guidance books we had to read.

That's what they were. The child guided the parents. Not that every mother really read Mr. Watson's book. Who had time? You had a cousin went to college or a neighbor took some courses, they told you what to do. Drove you crazy with rules your own mother, lucky woman, never heard of. The book, the dedication was "To the first mother who brings up a happy child." Such *chutzpah!*

Now, it's different. Self-demand means you can do anything you like, any time. If you call it a system, then you're not being sloppy. If Dr. Spock says it's O.K., then you're not a *shlump*.

Now there's a brand-new idea. Every baby is born "programmed" for life. This means that it doesn't make a hell of a lot of difference what you do. If he's going to be a great scientist or an ambassador or a murderer, there isn't anything can change it.

I don't know which idea is worse, this, or Watson's. But I know, from looking around, that the parents today are more relaxed than we used to be.

Everything now is disposable—diapers, jars from baby food, plastic bottles. Sometimes, I get in a mood, I wish they'd invent disposable parents.

No matter how many books you read, then or now, one thing is for sure. Just like with a landlord. The same for mothers or fathers. There's no such thing as a good one. But grandparents, I don't know how it happens, they're different. Way up on top, even *consulted,* sometimes. Even a landlord gets to be loved by his grandchildren.

You take three children to the supermarket, they fight for rides in the cart, they get all mixed up with Wheaties and frozen fish and Pepsi, who has the time to think of other troubles?

You can get through the day better, maybe get through life easier, if you just make up your mind that everything is *supposed* to go wrong.

"Some days," I say, "I'm going batty. I feel like I'm just falling apart."

"So you ought to be recycled," says smart-aleck Jeremy.

Maybe a neighbor comes along with *her* grand-children. Everybody admires, both grandmothers lie like hell. Anybody can see hers are not at all good-looking, anyhow.

One man, he should live to a hundred and twenty, he smiles at me and says, "Those are lovely children you have."

Six-year-old, not so lovely, speaks up. "She's not my mother," he says. "She's my grandmother."

The man laughs. "And my wife says I'm not tactful."

The children grab things off the shelves you don't need. Things that used to be bad for their parents—frankfurters, sausages, mustard. You wouldn't have let your own children even *smell* a pickle. Be educational. Buy flour and baking soda and things your daughter will never use up, and teach the children that waffles aren't born frozen.

The children scream, "I'm starving. I haven't had anything to eat all day."

Don't argue, give in. Buy the ice cream and the pizza even if it's before supper.

So who has time for getting blue and worrying about the Arabs?

Once I found a penny on the floor near the check-out counter. All the children clamored, "Give it to me, Grandma."

"No," I explained, "this, I keep. It's for good luck."

"Oh, I didn't know," Sebastian, so superior, says, "that you're superstitious."

"I'm not. It's just that it always works."

"You mean whenever you find a penny, something wonderful happens?"

"Sure, only last week I found one."

"What happened?" All children so attentive suddenly.

"Well, everything came up roses. In New York there were no forest fires, no earthquakes, no tigers at the door. You see what a good-luck penny can do."

Then with the homework I have to help. First

64

Jeremy's arithmetic, then Jessica has to memorize a poem. I have to hear her.

"Where are the snows of yesteryear?" she starts.

You ask a silly question, and if you're some kind of villain, a poet, and a bum, you get no answer. Any four-year-old knows what happened to last year's snow. It got filthy with gas fumes and pieces of old newspapers and cigarette butts and some of it melted and some was swished around by some kind of big machines that wore it out pushing it from one side of the street to another.

Then comes Sebastian's spelling I have to test him. To hear spelling, even if you're a teacher, you don't have to know how to spell. The words are right before you. Altogether I learn a lot.

One evening, very quiet like, the younger children busy writing letters to Santa Claus. So Jeremy, wise guy, says, "Christmas mail is slow. So you know what you kids should do?"

"What?"

"Send the letters straight to Grandpa Harry."

"Why to him?"

Quick, before Mr. Smarty Pants with another wise crack, I explain, "After Grandpa Harry retired, he took a job as Santa's helper."

"Oh," Jeremy helps out, "you know, like Hamburger

Helper." I said I'd mail the letters. They didn't need stamps.

Nowadays, you're allowed to relax with children; with the baby especially, it's a pleasure. You're allowed to pick up the baby, kiss, hug, say "Grandma's sweetie pie, my apple dumpling, honeybun," everything full of calories. But sometimes the noise, the arguments, make you wish for a jukebox. The kind where you put a dime in and get five minutes of silence. American children— everyone born a member of a debating team.

Kids full of complaints. Colin groans, "One or two little sneezes and all of a sudden I'm in bed full of chicken soup and all my clothes are gone into the washing machine."

"And what's more," Jeremy, that little *momser* says, "Grandma can't remember whether you starve a cold or feed a fever, so to be on the safe side, she feeds 'em both."

Jessica moaning to high heaven. "Why can't I have a party Saturday without a chaperone? A warden, I mean."

"Because you're only fourteen and someone should be around. I'm not here only to bring in the food."

Ten kids invited. Thirty-six came. Usually, when news gets around someone's giving a party, and my granddaughter's invited, five hundred of her most intimate friends turn up to escort her.

Plenty of Cokes and potato chips, no problem. But the dirty looks I got from thirty-six faces all evening was nobody's business. This showed how I cramped their style. I'm always glad to be needed.

By eleven o'clock, everyone left except two girls with sleeping bags staying overnight on the floor in the living room. I went to bed. Satisfied.

At midnight I thought I heard laughing, I went to the living room. About ten boys and girls came back. Must have been arranged, secret-like, with signals from the window when I went to bed.

Very angry, I threw them all out on their ears. Next day I waited for Jessica to say, "Grandma, you ruined my party." But no! All I heard was, "Gee, there were piles of kids I never saw before. Glad you ordered enough doughnuts and things." This, from Miss Guilty. But still, I'm good and sore at Jessica.

One thing I'll give credit to Dr. Spock. He says, right out, that you don't have to love your children twenty-four hours a day. This goes for grandmothers, too.

14

How to Make Money Out of Grandchildren

There are lots of good reasons for taking a baby to the park. At least one person will make a mistake and think you are the mother. When you say, "No, I'm the grandmother," she squeals, surprised, and you become lifelong bosom friends, for an hour.

Once, when my daughter, Elana, age forty, and I were together, one of the park benchers looked at me and said, to be complimentary, "You don't look a day older than your daughter." You should have seen the color of Elana's face. It matched the green fabric she was choosing to reupholster the couch.

One other item upset her. Sometimes, I lent her my senior citizen bus pass. Usually, bus conductors don't notice people, and she kept getting away with half fare. This, she wasn't happy about, but her economy was.

But once, a conductor looked at her face. "You sure don't look like a senior citizen."

Quick, my Elana. "That's because I had my face lifted," she smiles sweetly. Conductor gave her a look you could put in a Boris Karloff movie. But no argument.

In the park there are all the old ladies that look into the white carriage you bought for the baby, darling little Gideon.

"How old?"

"Three months."

"My grandson is three months. But he's bigger. Much bigger."

Sometimes they only admire. "So beautiful. *Kein ahurra.*"

"You ought to register him with a model agency."

My daughter, Elana, and her husband were still on vacation, so how could I ask permission? I went home, looked in the Yellow Pages, my fingers walking, and picked out "Model Personnel." Dressed the baby, took a cab, and felt like I was going on an adventure into darkest Africa. Nobody I know ever did such a thing before.

The office was filled with mothers who thought of it before. Children, all ages, most of them noisy, being scolded, slapped. They were called, one by one, looked at by a lady in a green suit (already I didn't like her), and sent away.

My turn with Gideon. She looked, gives out an order to me. "Remove all his clothes."

My heart stopped, but I said to myself, "Immoral it's not."

Gideon, nude, happy, on a table, and the green-knit-suit lady (I liked her better now), was writing down all sorts of things I hoped weren't going to the CIA.

"Now," she says, "you'll have to get the baby a social security number, a work permit, and a doctor's certificate. "This"—now she smiled—"is the start of his résumé."

Lucky, I thought, the parents aren't due back for about two weeks yet. A week later, "Model Personnel" phoned.

"We need a baby three months old. I see from the records your Gideon is just about that." State law, I found out, doesn't allow babies under three months to work. That would be child labor.

"Yes," I say into the phone, delirious without breathing, "just three months tomorrow."

"Is he small or big for his age?"

"Oh, big," me, the grandmother brags, "very big."

"Sorry," says the telephone voice, "we need a small one," and there was a click I'll never forget. What it did to my stomach is nobody's business. I wished the whole telephone company would go out of business.

Three days later, while I was running water for Gideon's bath, the telephone rang again. The maid called me.

"Model Personnel speaking. Bring that baby down right away for a sitting."

This was one bath that baby never got. I grabbed the baby, my purse, a half-empty bottle of milk, and rushed out for a taxi. Only an hour, Gideon was posed, photographed, posed again, photographed again, and back home.

Two days later, in the mail, comes a check for thirty-three dollars. Three dollars off for the agent. Now Gideon, three months old, was self-supporting. Before that, just a bum.

The parents didn't scold me at all. One look at the check, they were delighted, told all the friends.

"Does he have to join a union?"

"No, it's not a steady job."

Everybody hugged and kissed the little breadwinner.

I asked, "Are you going to start a special account for him at the bank?"

"Not at the bank," says my son-in-law. "At the A&P. Called a baby-food investment."

"What's the name of the model agency?" Someone asks.

"I'll tell my daughter-in-law to take her children down."

My friend Sarah means that *her* grandchildren are more beautiful.

"Pure commercialism," says one friend who's been hoping for years for at least one grandchild. "I'd never exploit a child like that." That woman, I wished that moment, would turn into a statue. And the pigeons shouldn't be constipated.

"The baby," I explained, "just does natural things—smiles, frowns, cries, everything except soiling the diaper—and gets thirty dollars an hour." *Their* grandchildren were smiling, frowning, crying their heads off, all for free. One nice thing about babies. They're always sincere. Not worried about their damn image.

A month later, I announce to every jealous busybody, "Gideon's price is up to thirty-five an hour, take off the agent's fee!" I speak now like I'm talking about a celebrity. "Last week alone he made over a hundred dollars." So maybe I exaggerate a little. The strict truth is never interesting, so why bother with it?

"Lots of cute babies," someone says, "grow into ugly

children. At the age of one year he could be a *has-been*."

"You see any ugly grandchildren in *my* family? They're considering," I say, "making a television test." *Too* much honesty. Who needs it? It's not good for the country, it's not good for General Motors.

15

Respect, That's for Grandmothers

My beautiful, blond hair-to-the-shoulder grandson Sebastian (his mother is musical, from Bach) used to measure himself against me. At age twelve, we were the same height, without my four-inch heels. My generation only took cod-liver oil. But not every child, only the skinny ones. We didn't grow as much as these kids with their tiny bugs in the pills called vitamins, and their junk food that's supposed to be so bad for them they should, by rights, turn out to be dwarfs.

By the time he was *bar mitzvahed* he was calling me "Shortie."

"Respect!" I say, trying not to laugh. My father used to say about *his* father, "So much respect we had, when he came into the room, we trembled."

Scared I don't want from my grandchildren, but now and then, believe me, a tiny bit of trembling shouldn't hurt.

So when Sebastian got real tall and didn't even have to ask me to take off my platform shoes anymore to measure himself by, one day he says, "Grandma, I'm not going to call you Shortie anymore."

He smiled, and came over and kissed me, and it wasn't even my birthday. From this I got suspicious.

"Good!" says I, but careful-like.

"Yup," he laughs. "From now on I'm going to call you Shrimpy."

A year later, everything became upside down. You know what he calls me now?

"Empire State Building."

Has he got a peculiar sense of humor? Now I ask you, whoever heard of anyone, no less a grandson, giving his grandmother, for her birthday, a belly-button brush?

He got it out of one of those mail-order catalogues. I saw the blurb—For those who have everything. Rhinestone-studded brush in a velvet-lined case. Removes navel lint. Sparkles elegantly as you use it. Reduced from $1.49 to 88¢.

When he gave it to me, Harry didn't even have the decency to look surprised. In his eyes was a very suspicious, elegant sparkle.

A belly-button brush! And, I ask you, who told Sebastian I had lint in my navel?

16

Diplomatic Relations with the Other Grandma

Don't tell your *machuteneste* that her daughter never had it so good. Tell your friend Frieda. She's not close-mouthed.

"What with a maid every day, with a decorator who bought expensive tshatchkes my own mother put on the dumbwaiter fifty years ago, with a doorman, an elevator man—she's used to it from home? My son doesn't let her dip her finger in cold water. In hot water for dirty dishes, for scrubbing the kitchen floor, this she never heard of."

Privately, I say to myself, what can you do with cold water except drink it?

"True," I say to Frieda, "she went to college, Radcliffe. A schoolteacher she's not—she sleeps till eleven—my own daughter should be so lucky."

The Other Grandmother tells you often, "My Mamie, I mean Melanie, you should see the boys that chased her, with white Cadillacs. She could have married a millionaire."

"So why didn't she?" I answer. My son, the girls *he* could have married, with money, from *really* good families. From the day he entered medical school, no, from the day he was *accepted* in medical school, my phone didn't stop ringing with propositions. Honorable ones, I mean. The other kind, he could make himself. He's no slouch in that department. Not that he was a run-around. But even Ivory Soap isn't 100 percent pure. So he had to go and fall in love. Who needs it?

"My Melanie, a natural blonde, so beautiful, she could have been Miss America."

"So why wasn't she?" you ask.

"Because the judges were anti-Semitic!"

"Many of the judges were Jewish."

"They're the worst kind. Only *shiksas* they like."

"Good-looking," you admit grudgingly, "she is. Even though her hair isn't natural. But cook she can't. Time was, a girl got engaged, her mother taught her how to cook. All you taught Melanie was how to thaw."

"To thaw? Like snow, you mean, when it gets warm?"

"Yeah! Right from the freezer."

"Oh."

"And you taught her another thing. Very important. To give a transfusion."

"A transfusion? What do you mean?"

"Like from a tea bag to hot water. Or a spoonful of instant coffee to a cup of water."

"Oh," she says again, relieved.

Don't go on with it. Better to tell your friends. "Sew she can't. Clean the house, she never heard of it. Only the beauty parlor she heard of. Saks Fifth Avenue, she heard of. To read books on how to bring up children, this she has time for. But to spend time with the children, for this she's too busy. My son, he's an angel. I can't say a word to him about her. I tell you, that Melanie fell into gravy."

But your son is happy. So what? Happiness isn't everything.

Always tell your grandchildren what a fine family they came from. Especially the ancestors that are dead. Maybe they weren't always so great, and maybe the children get a little bored, but if you don't keep up, the

Other Grandmother will get ahead of you, maybe digs up a doctor or a famous rabbi, but always in the old country.

She quotes them: "As my cousin Leon always used to say . . ." and she goes on and on, so you wonder. When he was alive, did anyone listen to what he always used to say? And how often did he say it? And what's so important about it anyhow, except that he's dead?

One day, Shira was busy making a genealogy chart. Asked a lot of questions, Aunt this, Uncle that, how many children, who married, why, when?

"Have we a family crest?" she asks.

"No," speaks up Jeremy, "just a lot of family crust."

"My father," I tell my grandson, "a very fine man, would be one hundred and thirteen years old if he were alive today."

"If your father were alive today," he answers me, "he'd be dead anyhow."

17

Thank God
for the Population Explosion

Big rewards come when grandchildren are three, four, and five years old. That's when you get lots of information from them; you hear details about their parents' quarrels. If they tell you something horrible about your daughter or son, don't believe a word of it. Children have such imaginations! But if they tell you something nasty about your daughter-in-law, think about it.

Baby-sitting is an important part of education. Not for them; for you. It is your duty, as soon as you are left alone with them, to ask them plenty of questions about the running of the household and their parents' private lives.

You need one trained spy in each family. Four to five years old is good. Seven is too late; they've already been hollered at not to talk so much. Besides, by that time they've become counterspies. Double-agent Arlene is one.

Pay careful attention. You'll hear about pending divorces among the parents' generation; about juicy fights in the family of the *machutunim*. You learn about proposed expenditures for new cars, summer cottages, new furniture. When a grandchild of three points to her stomach and says, "I want to have a baby here like Mommy," you find out that your daughter-in-law is pregnant.

You hear, "Daddy got up in the middle of the night and went to sleep on the couch in the living room. Grandma, what's a blond tramp?"

You answer circumspectly. "A tramp is a ship that carries freight. Blond means a light color, like hair or wood."

Your grandson seems a bit confused. "You mean Mommy was angry because Daddy was dancing all evening with a ship?"

There is much advance information as well as private analyses.

About various illnesses in all the branches of both

families, you've already heard: the fallen wombs; the prostates; different kinds of rocks and stones—kidney and gall; and varieties of blood pressure, like an electric appliance—high, medium, and low. Sickness is like stereo: You hear it from all sides.

Phone the children often, especially at such times as you know the parents aren't at home. And never, never, by so much as a hint, a word, or a glance indicate to the parents that you got plenty information they themselves didn't give you. It might result in censorship and interference with civil liberties, and this isn't the American Way of Life.

And the more grandchildren you acquire, the bigger the ways of getting information. When you have five or six lovely grandchildren, don't worry about any such nonsense like stopping the population explosion. That's for the *goyim*.

Spacing of children, yes, that I agree. But not what my husband Harry says after a day at my house with the grandchildren.

"Sure they should be spaced. About a mile and a half apart."

"But," you argue, "children brighten up the whole house."

"Yes," agrees my Harry, "they sure do. They leave all the lights on."

18

Some of Your Best Friends Are Not Grandmothers

If your daughter asks you to go along for a weekend at an expensive place her friend from Southampton recommended, and suggests that you and Grandpa Harry share a bedroom with little Jeremy, feel happy that she wants you.

That doesn't mean she won't transmit complaints:

Her husband doesn't like to share a bathroom with you.

He doesn't like to eat all his meals at the same place, and he doesn't like such paper-thin walls through which he can hear his son at six in the morning.

Why didn't you take the baby out for a walk?

If you have a husband, and take him along, you get the complaints from the other side.

"Is this supposed to be a vacation?" Harry asks.

But a grandfather isn't a total loss. Arlene, at the age of four, explained to her friend. "A grandfather is a man grandmother. He goes for walks with small boys in the family and they talk about baseball and cement mixers and silly things like that."

When you get home and call up your best friend Frieda to complain, she'll ask you, "Why did you have the baby in your room? It's their baby."

"Oh, I didn't mind that; I liked it."

"Did they pay for your weekend?"

"Oh no." You are surprised, indignant. "I paid for them."

"What! I never heard of such a thing. You're certainly a sucker."

This is a woman you've known for so many years, you feel sometimes you're not really old enough to have been friends that long. Never trust a friend that tells you the truth. Trouble is, you need old friends, just not to look at. You're better off you don't wear your glasses. To see hairs on lips, wrinkles on face, moles on the chin. Who needs it? Sometimes, you wear your glasses to read a menu and suddenly you look at your friend opposite. Don't go home and look in the mirror, and don't read the obituary notices.

"Well, my son-in-law's a Ph.D." You sigh. But with me, all he says is, "It's warm today" or "It's windy." The kind of manners he has, he'd never get a job at a tollbooth where he has to say "Thank you" for eight hours a day.

About another little *tsuris* you don't have to tell her either. When your grandson asked his father to play chess and the father said he was too tired.

"So I'll play with you," I said.

"No, Grandma," says the seven-year-old, "it'll be too difficult for you."

But after all, your friend Frieda doesn't know how the grandchild cries when you leave. Who else would let him stick pencils into a hairdo that looks like the Tower of Pizza. Or, maybe it's late, and he knows, when you leave, he'll have to go to bed. Or he has to give back your earrings, those French chandeliers. So he cries.

When you were a young girl, what thrilled you? A love letter, yes?

Now what thrills you? A postcard from a grandchild. Or little Colin cries he wants to sleep with you.

Don't boast about anything to your friend. Just bring her along sometime for a visit so she can see for herself.

Meanwhile, just say, dignified-like, "You don't understand. After all, *you're* not a grandmother."

19

It's Not Fashionable to Marry Jews Anymore

So when my son Jason told me and his father he had an announcement to make, and we should sit down, did I get nauseated?

A dying disease?

A job in Japan?

Drafted into the army?

"I'm getting married," he told us. I looked at his face. There was more coming.

"She's a fine girl. Good family. Good education. Excellent character."

"Good," I said, kissing him. "When do we meet?" I was anxious for him to marry, but I was still nauseated.

"There's just one small item you'll have to get used to."

"So?" Now it's coming, the big blow.

"She just happens to be Gentile."

Plenty of my friends have Gentile sons-in-law and daughters-in-law, so used to it I was already. Nauseated I still was, but ready with the right answer.

"If you love her, it makes no difference to me and Dad." I'm proud of this to this very day. A fine girl is Cynthia.

Later Harry said to me, "I think we handled this very well. Didn't show any reaction."

I sighed, the liberated grandmother, "At least he didn't say he was marrying a man."

"If he had, the first question you'd ask would have been, 'Is he at least Jewish?'"

We've come a long way since Eddie Fisher married Debbie Reynolds and Jewish women on the benches on Broadway used to moan, "A shame. A nice Jewish boy throws himself away on a shiksa."

My own mother, *olav hasholem*, was such an orthodox Jew, doing the breast stroke over the candles every Friday night, that when my brother said he was going to marry a shiksa, she threatened to sit *shiva* for him, like he was dead. She used to say, "These shiksas get hold of our nice Jewish boys by sleeping with them." But us girls, I notice, were brought up to stay away from sleeping or we'd *lose* the man. Confusing, yes. But sex before, or no sex, everybody got married. The only conclusion I can see from this is that Gentile girls should sleep and Jewish girls shouldn't.

So my friends ask questions. "Did Cynthia's family make objections?"

"Oh no," I said, laughing. "They said Jason's very nice, for a Jewish boy."

Later, I figured out, what really upset them was the social thing. So different. They're from Philadelphia, Main Line. This has nothing to do with a bus route.

Troubles? Of course, like in any marriage. But not because of religion.

Some things are more important. Like air. Yes, I mean air. Does one want the window wide open at night? The other likes all the radiators hot. One likes a heating pad in the double bed. One is always too hot, sweats. One yells, "Shut that window, I'm freezing to death." The other screams, "I'm suffocating." Nine-year-old Noah says, quiet-like, "Shut that window and let one suffocate to death. Then open it and let the other freeze to death!" Does he get scolded? No! A child is *supposed* to show hostility.

So there should be before marriage tests about air. More important than a Wasserman, believe me.

Only sometimes my son, Jason, he's only human, he forgets what he reads in all those books. Once, I heard him, with my own ears, yell at Noah, "For God's sake, shut up."

And Noah, cool like a psychologist, ups and says, "That's no way to talk to a nine-year-old child."

Jason's children aren't half Jewish and half Gentile. They're whole children, not half and half, like cream. Except that half the time, like all the other grandchildren, they're adorable, and half the time they're brats.

So my other grandson Colin says to me, "Why do they call Jews the chosen people?"

"Because God Himself chose us for the best."

"You mean," asks Colin, "that God discriminates?"

"Well, sort of."

Age eight says, "The Civil Liberties Union ought to get after Him."

Sometimes my son says to people, "My wife isn't really Catholic, you know."

Then Cynthia speaks up. "I may not have been to mass for fifteen years, but I was born a Catholic and I'm still a Catholic."

So Jason says, "I know. I was born a Jew. I'm an avowed atheist, but I'm still a Jew."

And Harry says, "And if you converted to Catholicism, my son, you'd *still* be a Jew."

But, God forbid, Jason should say, "My wife is a Catholic."

Cynthia gets mad. "I haven't been to church in fifteen years. I'm *not* a Catholic."

Instead of a Catholic, better Jason should have married a Buddhist or a Hindu. It's so different, it would have been *chic*. But Cynthia, God bless her, turned out to be such a nice person that now I consider her Jewish.

Only Harry has to put in his cute two cents. "If he had to marry a Gentile, why didn't he pick out one that didn't have a history of diabetes in the family?"

Now what's a nice Jewish disease, like that, I ask you, doing in a good Gentile family?

When the first child was born, we asked, "What religion?"

"No religion," they said.

But I asked Jason private, "Won't your mother-in-law take the baby secretly to be baptized?"

He laughed. "A little water won't hurt the baby."

One friend I got, she calls herself a friend, always full of warnings. She has no children, by the way.

"Just wait," she says, "your grandchildren will be marrying Negroes."

"That's perfectly all right"—I fixed *her*, but good—

"then my great-grandchildren won't have to bother getting suntans. Besides," I said, "so what? He might still be a good Jew, like Sammy Davis, Junior." This guy figured, why settle for one handicap when he could just as easily have two?

From such worries a person could be constipated for a week.

Integration doesn't mean, like it used to, between religions. Now it means between skins. Cynthia says, "I wouldn't live in a neighborhood that wasn't integrated."

This means there has to be one high-class Negro family—a famous baseball player, a Hollywood star, someone so high up he feels superior to all the whites around.

But times change fast. It's nothing, positively nothing, these days, to marry a Gentile. You have to marry a Negro, then you're *really Somebody*.

Whenever a friend calls up and asks whether I have a nice girl for her brilliant, handsome, smart son, or a nice boy for her educated, beautiful daughter, it means the son or the daughter is already mixed up with a Gentile.

"Nobody," I sigh, "is marrying Jews anymore."

"No," says my Harry, "nobody but Gentiles."

20

Lay-awake Plans

Your granddaughters, the darlings, always wear expensive dresses, straight from Saks Fifth Avenue. The grandson's overalls, for wearing out the seat on the slide in the park, come from a fancy Madison Avenue little store. It has to be little to be expensive. In the presence of your grandchildren, admire these clothes. Also, do not complain about the way their parents throw out money.

Refer, like accidentally, to the amount of money they overpay when they buy hi-fi sets, color TVs, cars, washing machines, and deep freezes on the installment plan.

"In my day," you explain, "it was considered a sin

to buy something when you didn't have the money. Or," you add, "when the old one could be fixed."

Your son will answer sociologically out of the depths of all the degrees he is smothered under.

"But, Mother, if this procedure were changed, our whole economy would collapse."

"If your wife had the money to pay for her cerulean mink coat before she bought it, our country would go to the dogs?"

Never ask what you should buy for Gerald or Arlene, because you will be told. If the parents want one of those educational toys for six dollars, go to the five-and-ten and get something similar for ninety-eight cents. The child will have just as much fun ignoring it.

From these toys, carefully worked over by teams of psychologists, he's supposed to learn coordination, color, mechanical techniques, and all sorts of other relationships. He'll learn just as much from a red-handled eggbeater. Even more from mud and water and sand, and have more fun.

Every generation, I notice, the child likes better a pot, with a cover to take on and off, forks, spoons, boxes of old buttons, broken jewelry. If they asked the grandmothers for advice, the psychologists would be out of jobs.

All you need these days is Scotch tape. It mends the broken toys, the torn pictures, paper dolls, balloons, books. Stops tears. Mends a broken heart. Must have been invented by a grandmother.

All the psychologists warn the grandmothers: "Don't bring presents *every* time you come." They're afraid the child might say, "What did you bring me?" before he even says "Hello-o."

Well, I can tell you different. Be sure to bring something even if it's to eat—blintzes, strudel, chopped liver from the delicatessen, or frozen. You unfreeze and put in a jar. My mother, olav hasholem, called it by its right name and chopped it herself in a wooden bowl, *gehachte leber*. But my daughter-in-law, ever since they moved to the East Side, speaks only of "paté," comes in a small glass jar.

So bring something, no matter what you call it. Your son, poor fellow, will be saved at least for one day from being undernourished. Your daughter-in-law may complain, "But, Mother, it's so fattening." Give the proper answer. "So what's a little flesh?"

In the old days, they brought up the children with rules. "Do this. Do that!" They didn't always obey. But they thought they were supposed to. Now it's all topsy-turvy. The parents obey the children.

When I was young, children weren't supposed to have feelings. Young people didn't go around looking for their identity. Identity, shmidentity. We didn't know we didn't have it.

Now children have feelings. Lots and lots of feelings. Only the parents aren't supposed to have any.

Is this way better? Is it worse? Who knows? Now everybody, parents and children, look for identity. The result? *Everybody* has troubles. Some of these people looking for their identity, from what I can see of them, would be better off if they didn't find it.

If your son happens to be sick, one day, tell him never mind about antibiotics and all those medicines on TV that drop into the stomach like from a leaky faucet. A good plate of homemade soup will cure him. After all, you may not see it on the commercials, but what flows in the umbilical cord from a Jewish mother to a son? Chicken soup!

But for the grandchildren, bring drums, boomerangs, horns, whistles like the policeman uses.

Anything shrillingly noisy or items that knock down the furniture or fly into the bric-a-brac are what children enjoy most.

Never mind what the Other Grandmother brings.

You want a word of advice, how to have a good visit? Don't come with good news to your daughter like that the man she didn't marry just got a $45,000 job or that someone's son just got a scholarship for medical school.

Better you should tell her about Aunt Bessie's Parkinson's disease, about Mrs. Bloom's nephew that had a nervous breakdown, or lost a job, or had a big fight with his wife and took all the money out of the joint account.

You want a cheerful visit? Bring bad news.

21

Propaganda

When Gerald gets to be eleven years old, don't ask the parents if he's going to be bar mitzvahed. You've already heard from them on this subject—about principles, ignorance, superstition.

Talk to Gerald privately. Tell him about your friend —Mrs. Gerstein whose grandson had his name up in lights on the marquee where the bar mitzvah party was held.

"And the fountain in the middle of the room. with *borsht* flowing into the basin."

Get him all worked up about the party. "Your face and head standing on the table, a sculpture of chopped liver. By Sir Jacob Epstein. Well, so maybe he's dead.

We'll get Jacques Lipschitz." But what really gets his attention, though, is the large map of Israel, made entirely of chocolate and vanilla halvah, with nuts for the lakes.

Later on, there comes a time when it can be mentioned to Gerald's parents. The amount of presents that can be counted on should be emphasized. The English bicycle, chemical sets, cameras, watches, microscopes, and the money.

"Enough to get him a trip to Europe when he's older. Maybe a car."

The parents will ignore you.

Tell Gerald about the gala event itself. "An open book made out of gefüllte fish with the Ten Commandments written in red pepper."

You need not mention to him that you expect to invite all your friends. You've given their relatives presents for years; it's time they paid off. Besides, you owe quite a number of dinners. This will even things up for a while, especially the way they run these affairs now—it'll last a whole weekend.

For this party, they can't treat you like they did last year on New Year's Day. They asked you to do research (like you were maybe that lady who is headquarters of Consumer Affairs), to find out the cheapest and best chicken liver, best ham, fruit by the case. They asked for recipes you should give to the maid. They borrowed the copper coffee urn, the flat silver, it was my mother's, she'd turn in her grave, and the large Mexican fruit bowls. And then you weren't even invited to the party.

For bar mitzvahs, they have to show off as many grandparents as they can get.

Explain how they can keep the whole thing simple. You're not telling them to charter a plane to Israel and put everybody up at the King David like Sadie Beckstein's grandson. Very show-offy, if you ask me. And I'm not saying it just because I wasn't invited. Only close relatives, she told me. But I know for a fact, our friend Becky Safir was invited. Becky wasn't supposed to tell me, but she couldn't keep from bragging. Something simple will do, like the Waldorf Astoria or the Hilton.

Finally, when Gerald is twelve, and religious instruction must be started, it's time to explain to the parents that they can invite all their business associates and make it tax deductible.

"Besides, it's the last big expense for him. When he gets married, the girl's family pays for the wedding."

Your daughter-in-law, having had enough harassment from Gerald, will say, "But, Mother, we don't believe in that sort of superstition."

"Superstition!" you exclaim. "He'll collect thousands of dollars worth of presents and you call *that* superstition?"

22

Grandma Goes to Pot

When I was young, a few women just began to smoke. Remember the cigarette advertisement, a woman says to a man, "Blow some *my* way"? When I started smoking, I was called a hussy. Sometimes people would ask, "Do you smoke in front of your children?" If you were Danish, it was O.K. Then you could even smoke cigars.

But now, it's twelve years since I had my last cigarette. Arlene loves to tell the story how she made me stop smoking. Her mother left her with me for the weekend and when I was putting her to sleep in one of those grandmother cribs, the kind that folds up and can be stuck in a closet between visits, I started to sing a lullaby. First, "Mammy's Little Coal Black Rose" what you can't sing anymore or the NAACP will get after you. But I was so hoarse, I couldn't belt out a decent note. Then I tried something more high class, but even Brahms isn't a cough syrup for the throat.

So I decided, I better quit those two packs of Chesterfields every day, just a few weeks until my throat wasn't so scratchy. Twelve years it was, and I haven't had one since. Arlene, the darling, takes all the credit.

She often says, when there's company, "Grandma, tell how I made you stop smoking," and then she kisses me and says, "Now you owe me a lullaby."

Demand performance, and I have to sing a few snatches of "The Slumber Boat." "Baby's boat's the silver moon. . . ."

But cigarettes, that's old hat.

A backward grandma, I am not. So when I decide to try a marijauna cigarette, where do I go to get it? Not to my friends, the wrong generation, not to the supermarket, not to some shady character in the pizza parlor. But to a grandchild.

My husband, Harry, usually a man with broad views, begins to object. "Don't ask Arlene for pot. It'll only encourage her to smoke it."

"Surely," I answer, "she's tried it. Where do you think she' been living for fifteen years?"

"I'm telling you. It's immoral to let her think it's all right for a grandmother." Harry goes out and slams the door.

This means that I have to ask Arlene when Harry isn't around. Arlene seems surprised, but amused. "Of course," she explains, "I don't use pot. But I know one or two kids who'd know where to get it."

"Just one cigarette," I explain, "just to see what happens."

"Shall I smoke one with you?" Arlene asks. "Not that I've ever tried it before."

I'm a grandma that believes everything. Yeah, yeah. This is the granddaughter who tried to hide *Playgirl* when I came into the room.

"Never mind shoving that magazine under your behind," I said. "I can get a kick out of the pictures, too."

So I open the centerfold—all those pictures of men showing up so big, like zucchini squash. Only the color is different. Don't tell me—Is it silicone? Makes a woman married forty years wonder what she's been missing. I guess that's the whole point of publishing the magazine.

Growing up with my grandchildren, that's me all over, Mabel. Sometimes they make me feel I just reached adolescence.

More education comes. So one afternoon Arlene

phones me to come over. Several grandchildren and their friends all gathered together like for a press conference or a television show.

Arlene and her friends—they hardly ever *heard* of pot, mind you—gave me instructions. "Inhale it down to your toes!"

At first, nothing, like a Chesterfield which I gave up twelve years ago. A few more puffs, and I'm breathing deeply and all the audience watching and breathing deeply. Synchronizing with me.

Suddenly, I started to sing. And the song was "Some of These Days," which I never knew all the words of before. My voice got louder and fuller and "I'm Sophie Tucker," I belted out.

"Who's Sophie Tucker?"

I didn't bother to answer. God knows where the memory came from, but one of Sophie's jokes came to me. "It isn't the men in your life that counts, but the life in your men." For this the adolescents didn't need any of those new sex manuals.

And then, in fine form, I was singing, "Darling, *je vous aime beaucoup*," and I don't know any French.

"Hildegarde," I laughed.

"Who's Hildegarde?" This young generation is very backward.

Two more puffs of grass (I even learned what to call

it) and I was sitting on the Spanish shawl on top of the baby grand piano.

"When you cover a piano with a shawl," I laughed, "you want the piano to keep warm, it shouldn't get pneumonia. So what do you say to the piano?"

The children, by this time, were the best audience any performer at the Palace ever had.

"What do you say to the piano?" they asked, straight men.

"Wear it in good health." Now my windpipe was blasting off like a rocket to the moon. And that's where I was sitting. I was Jenny Lind, and believe me, I don't know any Swedish. But no nightingale trilled any trillier than me.

"Come, Josephine, in your flying machine, going up she goes, up she goes." Where all the words came from, I'll never know.

"Helen Morgan," I crooned from the top of the piano.

The children weren't even asking who those weird people were anymore. They were just laughing and kidding me, and the younger ones were rolling on the floor.

"Grandma, you're so funny!"

"Give the little girl a big hand," I begged.

"My hand's the biggest," says Gerald. "You want to

hold it?" By this time the kids weren't even expecting common sense.

Now I was expecting any minute the phone to ring, inviting me to team up with Pearl Bailey to sing at the White House.

"Your grandmother certainly is a good sport," Arlene's friends began discussing.

"*My* grandmother only knits." (And glad of it too.)

"Yours is so"—she hesitated—"colorful."

When I came to "Mairzy Doates and Dozey Doates" they thought I was so certifiable that I couldn't even remember real words.

Arlene began to look a little scared. "Maybe you better not smoke the rest of it, Grandma!"

"Ish kabibble," I shouted.

Sometimes, even without pot, I get mixed about time. I think I'm my own mother. Now I thought I was my own grandmother, that naïve woman who didn't know where her nine children came from. British, she wasn't (a thousand miles away in Poland), but she sure was Victorian.

"Twenty-three skiddoo," I said, just finishing the cigarette. "This, I call living. That's me all over, Mabel."

And then, who walks into that room, who was supposed to be playing golf, but my dear, hated husband, loving, nasty Harry. Believe me, if I could have dropped dead that minute, I'd have been the happiest woman alive.

But you know what? He sees the children laughing, he sees the cigarette in my fingers, and he just looks and looks and finally says, "For one afternoon I leave you, and what happens? You become a *grass* widow!"

23

Your Grandson, the Doctor

When your daughter threatens to throw herself out of the window, first of all you say, calm-like, "Don't be so quick with the suicide. You kill yourself, things get better and later you'd be sorry."

So you get to the point. "What did he do now?"

This refers, not to her husband, but to her son, a senior in high school, sending out applications for college.

Your daughter, weeping, tells you about the greatest disaster that can befall a Jewish mother.

"Jeremy says he won't even register for a premedical course."

You are a grandmother, mellowed with time, experienced in tragedy, a philosopher. You can remember other disasters, like when your daughter didn't want a wedding. She said it was a hollow symbol; you didn't have to broadcast to everybody you were going to bed. This, you knew damn well she had done already anyhow. You can remember other crises like when they didn't want to name the baby Lancelot after your grandfather Laben.

"Jeremy's got a right to make up his own mind." Show how many modern books you read. "He should be anything he wants. Tell him he can be any kind of a doctor he wants."

This is not the moment to tell her about your friend Mrs. Silverblatt's grandson, the urologist or proctologist, who knows what—something to do with a toilet—he charges fifty dollars for a consultation. Besides, who can believe everything Mrs. Silverblatt says, anyhow?

Don't tell your daughter now. Later, when she calms down, is time enough to get her nervous.

"Calvin," she says, "doesn't think a profession is important." Calvin is her husband. "He says that true happiness comes only from recognizing one's own imperfections and making a good adjustment to reality."

My son-in-law, God bless him, is a physicist who gets all kinds of money from foundations to study things he can't even explain. I wonder if Mr. Fulbright and Mr. Ford and Mr. Guggenheim know what he's doing. Educated, he is. Smart, he is not.

Me, I had no trouble with my son Winthrop. He was raised from a baby to be a doctor. And the pleasure Harry and I got from it. From the day he entered medical school, my relatives and friends started calling me up for medical advice. It was the same with my other son Jason, when he entered law school. The phone rang steadily. But on legal advice I wasn't good, because you can't learn much law from Perry Mason. One hour a week with Dr. Welby is as good as four years in medical school.

So try to soothe your daughter about her abnormal son.

"So let him be a dentist. A druggist, if necessary." Sigh heavily. "Many fine men have been dentists, God forbid!"

24

Florida Is an Old-age Home

Go live in Florida? Never!

"Now that Harry's retired," my friends say, "what do you need all this cold weather for? Snow, slush, boots, heavy coats, woolen panties."

One winter Harry and I spent in one of those sanitary villages with the fancy names—Grande Vista, Palmtree Court, Senior Joy. So sanitary it was, there wasn't anyone to look at that didn't make you feel old, just plain old. Not that I'm any spring chicken, but I don't want to be reminded so often.

In *Fiddler on the Roof,* remember when Tevye sings

how he doesn't know how his daughter got so grown-up? I know how my children grew. I watched. But who knows how *I* got so old? This I can't understand. This I should sing about? But who feels like singing? I think, sometimes, I'll wake up in the morning and I'll be the right age for me, say thirty-two, with young children to need me, and no television talky talky shows to *verdrehen mir ein kopf* "do the children love me, don't they love me?"

When they want to train dogs to be good-natured, they put them in homes where there are three generations. When I'm eighty, that's where they should put *me*.

In Florida, the only relief from card playing was when someone's daughter came down with the grandchildren for a week. A big favor they did the parents who had to bribe them with all kinds of promises besides the first-class air fare. All the seniors make such a fuss over the visiting children, you can see how they miss their own. Day and night.

The big deal every day is the mailman. Such worry for a letter or a measly post card. When you can't stand the worrying anymore, your husband gets mad at you.

"There's nothing to get worked up about," says Harry. "This happens whenever we travel."

Sure, when Harry's playing golf, he doesn't worry. When he's playing pinochle, he doesn't worry. In the classy sauna bath, no worries. Guzzling beer, very cheerful.

But me, all I got to do is sit and listen to talk about who said what to whom and shouldn't have, and boasting who has more children with professions, and whose children paid the most for their houses in Westchester or cooperatives in New York. This part I can handle. I can exaggerate as well as the next one.

Discussions, such deep discussions like it was philosophy, about restaurants and food and what they ate for lunch, as though anyone cares, and what to eat for dinner. And snacks in between, their stomachs shouldn't shrink between meals. Their minds, they already shrank long ago.

Sometimes the talk gets deep, very deep.

"You should do it now, not tomorrow."

"Tomorrow, all of a sudden, becomes today."

"Today was tomorrow yesterday."

"Yesterday was today when today was tomorrow."

"Even tomorrow will be yesterday sometime."

"Someday, every day will be tomorrow."

Weather takes up a lot conversation. What it is back home, what it was here yesterday. Some people take the weather personally. It got too cold, just to spite them; it rained, just to be mean to them.

My Harry says, one nice thing about becoming an elder statesman (no senior citizen for him!) is that you can say you don't want to do a lot of things, without explanations. You can say, "I don't want to go" or "I don't want to exert myself" or "I don't feel like it." Besides, you can sit down a lot.

"Really," he says, "we should be called Elder Jurists."

"Why?"

"Because we have nothing to do, so we sit around and judge everybody. Maliciously, of course."

Then there are the show-offs. Fourteen-carat bracelets with five grandchildren hanging from it, with names and birthdays engraved. "English Gothic," someone boasts. One woman, she jangles her bracelet, has the birthstone of each child on the charms. Another grandmother, the big four-flusher, has only diamonds.

Then there are the matchers. Not the ones, "Have I got a girl for you?" kind. No! These ones have a purse, have to spend days shopping to find a scarf to match. If you have a scarf, you shop to find gloves to match. Shoes, belts, everything to match.

"I'm tired."

"So why do you shop so much?"

"So I won't get depressed!"

"Depressed from what?"

"From not shopping."

Widows, widows galore. Women don't die anymore. Only men. Such struggling if a single man shows up, even if he's ninety years old and probably impotent.

With Parkinson's disease. Not that I don't feel sorry for them. Me, with my Harry, I'm stuck up. And believe me, I don't let him around loose.

Every morning, first thing before breakfast, the widows rush to read the obituary pages to line up the prospects. They get to them even before the banks seal the vaults. Then they hang around the widowers' mailboxes and invite them up for a drink.

Another topic conversation I can do without. Teeth. Everyone has special bragging.

"I have precision appliances." The word *dentures* you dassent use.

"My dentist is very particular about occlusion." This means the top should hit the bottom so you can bite a hot pastrami on pumpernickel.

"Five thousand dollars for the uppers alone I paid."

"Me. I have implants." Costs even more. Hoity-toity.

One thing is clear. The older the face, the younger the teeth.

But I miss the family. Always I have premonitions. If they don't happen, the premonitions don't count.

Every day I write postcards to one of them, always I must remember about not using Mrs. or Miss only Ms., so a woman shouldn't let the postman know she didn't catch a husband yet. The colored maids always call us "Miz" anyhow. They got there ahead of Women's Lib. Finally, I tell Harry, "Tonight at eight o'clock when the rates change I'll call Elana and find out what terrible things they are keeping from us."

"All right," he says, "but you don't have to talk to *each* grandchild."

After forty years, you don't argue. Like I always say to my daughter, "After so many years, I know how to handle your father."

"That's terrible," says Elana. "Marriage is not supposed to be a matter of manipulation. It should be co-operation."

"That's it," I explain. "I handle, he cooperates."

So, I go ahead and speak to each grandchild and to my daughter, Elana.

"Oh, Mother," she says, "we were just going to write."

A marvelous instinct I have, whether I'm in Florida, Paris, or Hong Kong. I always figure out to phone just the very day they were planning to write.

Then a grandchild asks to talk to Grandpa Harry. The expression on his face? Lit up like Times Square on New Year's Eve. Then I talk again. He fidgets. I hang up.

"I told you," says Harry, looking at his watch, figuring up the long-distance charges, "it was foolish to phone."

My husband, God bless him, will spend thousands on cruises to the Carribean, on airplanes to Japan, but a few dollars for a long-distance phone call gives him stomach cramps. Me, I'm just as dopey, only about different things. A book from the public library, over due, I'm still reading, paying ten cents a day, can give me nervous prostration.

You get older, you're supposed to get wiser. With age, also comes foolishness. Sometimes foolishness is better. On Sunday, I don't announce out loud, I'm going to phone another set of grandchildren. The third set, sometime when Harry's off fishing, even at full rates. Before the phone call I was so depressed I wouldn't have smiled if I were on candid camera.

So bored does everybody get that they even have religious discussions. If you say you're an atheist, someone asks, "A Jewish atheist or a Christian atheist?"

If you don't go to a temple or a church, you aren't trusted. Someone's bound to try to get you to become a Scientist. Not a physicist or a chemist. A Scientific Christian, the kind that doesn't go to doctors. Only faith you should have. From faith, my son, the doctor, wouldn't have to pay *any* income taxes.

"God loves you." They have inside information, maybe?

"If God loved us, He wouldn't have created us," my Harry answers, making some brand-new enemies.

And then, when the women are alone, there are those big confidences about the men they could have married. Only after thirty or forty years does a woman really know which one that was dying to marry her she should have picked. He's the one that became a millionaire. Was there ever any woman on this earth that married the right man?

I can't compete on this one. As Harry says to me, "I didn't hear of any suicides from your old boyfriends."

Every now and then, you get annoyed with your husband, you look around and figure, "Believe me, if I'd had any sense, I could've done better."

But after forty-five years, you get some different ideas. You look at your husband, you look at other husbands, and you think, "Believe me, I coulda done a lot worse."

Besides, you remember when you were young, hunting around for good prospects (never admitted it, of course, even to your girl friends, only to your mother; she was getting nervous since you were sixteen years old), the best men were already married. Funny thing, some men seem to have been *born* married.

Then there are the second marriages. They always look so peaceful. The wife raves about how wonderful the husband is. This, you'll remember, is the husband the first wife (dead or divorced, maybe murdered!) found so difficult, maybe horrible, impossible to live with. So I look at Harry, the man I sometimes quarrel with, sometimes hate, and I think, "If I die or divorce him, his next wife will think he's a saint." For this alone, I decide, I won't die first.

Operations, no end. If you didn't have one of these hysterectomy things cut out, or at least a gallbladder, you aren't a member of the community. When a man comes to sit down at the swimming pool, you know already from his wife if he has trouble taking a leak, or if he had already a prostate and pees like a horse.

Some days you could write up each person's bowel movements and put it on a chart. One lady, she had the runs so many days, my Harry started saying, "There goes a loose woman."

"Nobody knows," she moans, "what I suffer." If they don't, they must be stone deaf.

Another one had a long story, full of details, about how she had a terrible gallbladder attack in a department store while she was looking at digital watches.

"They had to call an ambulance. Right there at Ohrbach's, it happened."

After she told the story three times, she heard someone remark, "A person goes to a store like Ohrbach's, anything can happen."

Next time she told it, it happened in Altman's. The story got promoted in stages—from Saks Fifth Avenue to Gucci's to Bergdorf's. The attacks got worse, the locations got better. By the end of the Florida season, it was a very classy gallbladder. It happened at Tiffany's.

"I almost died," she moans. Euthanasia, I'd recommend.

That woman cried when she was born and they slapped her behind. And she hasn't stopped since. To give a good *potch* in the same place would be a pleasure.

Reminds me of the time Pope John gave out a *pacem in terris*. The first word pronounced like the Yiddish potch. Lots of good it did. Nothing but wars ever since. Better he should have issued a potch'em in *tuchis* to all the big shots.

Experts! Everyone a specialist. Mrs. Segal's husband has a pacemaker; she knows more about heart surgery than Dr. De Bakey.

Mrs. Brook has a cousin had a heart transplant. "Much better than a pacemaker."

Arguments, like everybody went to medical school. "A by-pass operation," says Mrs. Berg, "is the best." Any hour of the day you can get a second opinion.

Mrs. Newman had a sister went to Mexico last winter, so if you have anything wrong in the intestines, she prescribes for you. One woman knows all about high blood pressure, tells you not to bother to go for tests, she'll tell you what to do about salt. Another is a high-class specialist on kidney stones.

Psychiatry. Dozens of analyzers around the pool. All free, too. Specialists of specialists. Mrs. Geiger knows everything there is to know about male menopause. In this community, most men wish they were back there suffering the forty-year-old symptoms.

And for bowels—they move, they don't move, you can get free consultations from the best medical opinions. We have authorities on backaches, kidney stones, sinus trouble, you name it. We even have a faith healer. You listen carefully, you can save a fortune on doctor bills.

Most evenings, unless you go to a movie, get very boring. All you do is wait for the eleven o'clock news so you can go to bed. They ought to run the late news like soap operas: Let the good guys win and give us all a comfortable night's sleep.

Two things, especially in Florida, get very monotonous. The noise of the ocean waves you can't shut off, and mink stoles. And those other noises—birds making a racket wakes you up at six o'clock, trees hustling in the wind, frogs croaking, like they have sore throats, supposed to be a beautiful sound, all full of things for learning poetry by heart. But for me, not the right kind of noises.

The worst torture you have to stand is all those snapshots of everybody's grandchildren passed around all day.

You sit down on a bench in the park, or at the pool, a strange woman next to you says, "It's a nice day."

But what she means is, "How many grandchildren you got?"

So the conversation begins. . . .

"Do you baby-sit?"

"How old are they?"

"Do you have trouble with your daughters-in-law?" The best ones, you notice, are the ones living in California or Italy or someplace faraway.

"What do your sons do?"

"Families are large these days. Before I get done, I expect to have eight or nine."

"Here are the pictures."

"This is Linda, age three. She signed her name. Her father teaches in a university. Oregon."

"This one is Bruce. A regular Gregory Peck. And smart!" The "little geniuses" are always the ones closest to home.

"Here are the twins. See the pagoda back there? They're in Bangkok. My son is in the State Department." Next time I meet this woman she'll call him an ambassador.

"Well, I'd rather be the grandmother of eight than the mother."

To find out what each relative does, you got to listen, but careful.

"My son-in-law's an educator," means he's only a schoolteacher.

"My daughter's a sociologist" can mean she has a lousy job as a social worker with the welfare department.

Other women say, "My son, Melvin," or "My daughter, Diane," but if the son's a doctor or a dentist, it's always, "My son, *Dr.* Finklestein."

"Merchant" is simple. It means he doesn't have a profession and didn't get his job from going to that school at Harvard that teaches you what my Harry learned about business all by himself and did good at.

Another thing annoying. All those baby stores. Big signs outside say, "God Bless Grandparents." One had a sign, "Welcome Grandparents," like a convention. Maybe if you buy, you get a label to wear. And the things they make you buy, special kind for girls, different for boys. Not just the colors. God forbid you should put a cap with a little brim on a boy. A boy, an infant, mind you, can't wear a dress when he's one-week-old. He might become homogenized or something. When it says on front of the sweater "I love Grandma," it costs three times more.

But the reason all these stores bother me, to tell the truth, is because I buy, I send; with three sets of grandchildren, every minute there's a birthday or some *mishugane* kind of graduation—from sixth grade to junior high, from kindergarten to first grade, with tiny white caps and gowns yet; there's Halloween, there's Thanksgiving. Not only family birthdays, I have to worry about Mr. Lincoln and Mr. Washington. They have birthdays, too. And do I even get a thank-you card all written out by Hallmark, such fancy words, only to sign the name?

One lady at the pool pulls out a great big card, passes around, "Smell," she orders. You open, a big bouquet of paper violets hits you in the eye. It smells, too. "From your loving granddaughter, Agatha," it says.

"Four months old," the happy grandmother says. "She adores me."

Another lady, can't stand it, says, "Commercialism, these cards. It's nauseating."

"Yeah, yeah," says I. "When you don't get one, that's what you get nauseated from."

Those efficiency apartments, all alike, only one has blue tiles in the bathroom, the other has green; they have everything for old-age comfort. Everything except what you want most. And that's *Obligations*, the things you don't want to do, you complain maybe, but you do them.

One morning I was walking on Lincoln Road and, suddenly, a downpour. A young girl in a long red sackcloth sack, one of those freaks, stops, raises her hands and arms and looks up at the sky, her face dripping wet.

"Thank you, Jesus, for the rain," she hollers.

Now I ask you. Is this fair? The guy's been dead two thousand years and folks are still thanking Him. Me? I send the grandchildren birthday checks, do I even get a lousy thank-you card? Me, I'm alive and dead, living in Florida. Better I should stay home with the wind and the head colds and keep track of what's going on in everybody's home.

25

The New-time Religion

With religion, every generation has trouble. From way back. A son won't learn Hebrew. A daughter gets married, won't light candles Friday night. But the trouble we have from my grandson Gerald, seventeen years old, it should happen *only* to a dog.

First, he's a fallout from high school. Then he leaves a good home, his own room and bath with all the pennants on the wall, and goes to live in a commune on East Fifth Street and eats only rice and yoghurt, plain.

What his parents tell him, he doesn't hear. Only what his guru says, that he listens to.

"In India," says Winthrop, Gerald's father, "there's a guru on every corner. And every guru has a guru.

There's too much competition, so the smart ones come over here."

When he comes to visit, always he brings along other mishugoyim, boys with hair all shaved off, girls dressed in saris. After a good meal, pot roast, corn fritters, *luckshon* pudding, the youngsters try to sell us pamphlets explaining everything, how they're "taking knowledge," they should find out "the whole universe is one great field of energy."

Energy from the rice they eat they haven't got. Very thin, all of them. Gerald had his head all shaved off except for a long pigtail in back like the old Chinese laundrymen who used to give us children two lichee nuts when you brought the bundle. Baldheaded like Yul Brynner, he doesn't look. Baldheaded like some eagle we're supposed to save, yes. If the bald eagle looks like Gerald and all his friends, it's not worth saving.

"How much for the pamphlet?" I ask, getting out my purse.

"The mahatma doesn't set a price. He's not interested in money," says his friend, the one wearing a leather belt with a buckle shaped like a penis.

"O.K.," I say to Sri Chinaraham (that's my Jewish grandson used to be named Gerald). "Here's ten dollars. Use it for yourself, maybe a pair of jeans without holes. It's not for gasoline for your mahatma's Rolls Royce."

Gerald looks like a pain he has in his bowels, but he takes the money and caresses his love beads.

A grandmother is supposed to give from the heart. My heart felt as lumpy as a glob of sour dough. Even if I beheld a rainbow in the sky it wouldn't help; nothing would leap up. Outside on the street, by Bloomingdale's, they sell the pamphlets for thirty-five cents. Outside Lord and Taylor's, some other bunch of crazies jump up and down, singing something and collecting money for someone named Harry Krishner. Sounds Jewish to me, so I gave a quarter.

So much love and brotherhood they're oozing, makes you wish for a little hatred, the old-fashioned, familiar kind. The conversation, though, isn't always what you call full of brotherly love.

Sometimes Gerald brings along a girl, name's Rosemary, only now she don't hear unless you call her Sidriha. Her I know since she's in diapers. She was cleaner then. Now she wears sandals with thongs over dirty toenails. Her grandmother is my good friend, Beatrice.

At lunch, over hot pastrami sandwiches, Beatrice and I talk. We're not happy.

"So now," I say, "your Rosemary, I almost didn't recognize last night. Instead of her beautiful blond hair, she wears a great big African bushy thing, looks like the inside of a hair mattress. To be white, it's not fashionable anymore."

"All I hope," says this grandmother, "is that she will take a bath when she comes home to visit."

We grandmothers, like it or not, have to learn to take life as it comes. That means, most of the time, to shut up. And be miserable. Life? Sometimes it's good, sometimes it's bad, but I wouldn't have wanted to miss it for all the tea in China. Besides, who can drink all that tea?

Sometimes, Gerald and his friends do some exercises on the living-room floor.

"This," they explain, "gives us divine bliss." The same thing in a YMHA gym would give a Charley horse. Then they show us how to make yourself so happy you could float on air.

"Press on your eyeballs, put your fingers in your ears, press your tongue back in your throat, and presto— Divine Bliss—out."

Sidriha sits on the floor, something called lotus position (like the old-time tailors), and begins to sway. "I feel my head expanding with light. I find myself entering a beautiful, luminous world. My whole being seems to rise up from the depths of my chest and I feel like I'm floating on some calm, endless ocean, unaware of my physical body."

This is what happens to the physical body when you only eat rice every day. Also, what happens when you smoke grass, not the kind you cut with a lawnmower.

Gerald's mother, Melanie, and I visited this commune where all the disciples, about twelve boys and girls, sleep in one big loft. Cold. One measly toilet in the hall. Windows so dirty you can't see the view. Better that way, anyhow.

So here, on the filthy wooden floor, a bunch of kids were rolling, twisting, shrieking like animals, making like banshees.

"They're having labor pains, maybe?"

"No," explains Gerald, "they're working up to a cosmic primal scream."

They're sure working up to something, I think.

The beds all have to face one way, something to do with getting the right vibrations from the earth's axle. When they bring visitors, they sleep on the floor, but north to south, or something. It changes with the moon.

"So why," Melanie asks, "don't you all go up to Tarrytown and live in that half-a-million-dollar estate with your guru?"

"We don't care about material things."

"Only the guru cares about them?" I ask.

Gerald looks at me like I'm retarded. "He enjoys the luxuries to a certain extent, but if he didn't have them, it wouldn't matter. The Knowledge is what counts. His highly developed consciousness enters our unillumined mind and actually lifts our consciousness. He guides us through the inner circuits of our psyche to the God that is within."

Then he sells me another pamphlet for ten dollars.

Beatrice and I have so many lunches together we're eating, not cheese blintzes only, we're eating our hearts out. Funny, we've been friends thirty years, and we never had much in common before. One thing we have in common now is the weight we're putting on.

"Wouldn't you think, Beatrice, that if you buy an expensive scale at Hammacher and Schlemmer, they'd guarantee it wouldn't register any increase in weight?"

"In one way," says Beatrice, "we're still lucky. How long it'll last, only God knows."

"How do you mean, lucky?"

"Well," she explains, "you know Becky's grandson? Belongs to some other community cold-water flat. I think it's called Yen Buddhism, or something. Means he has a yen to go to Japan. So he and a girl friend, mind you, are starting out with knapsacks on their backs, full of pots and knives and forks and blankets, and they're going to fly part way and hitchhike the rest."

"Where did they get the money? Don't tell me their parents are giving it."

"No, the boy has his bar mitzvah money still in the bank. Saved for college. They have to go to 'The Supreme Worship Object' at Mount Fuji, straight to the Source."

"The source of what?" I asked, so ignorant.

"Who knows what? They chant a lot."

So many lunches we have, now I call us The Hot Pastrami Friends. The telephone company makes a good profit on us, too.

This morning, after hearing Melanie on the phone with a mother's complaints, I call Beatrice, with the latest news.

"Now I hear they're eating only Yin and Yen."

"What's that, a new kind of breakfast cereal?"

"No, it's something about balancing the food for a balanced brain. It's got a name something like macro-idiotic. It may balance Gerald, but believe me, his mother is all unbalanced."

"My idiot granddaughter," says Beatrice, "is trying to reach an absolute state of self-assertion."

"What's that?"

"Do you think I know? You get it by sitting on the floor with your feet under your behind. She says she's getting good results. Her guru, in India, sent her a new name. What she needs more than a new name is a new bra. Her bosom is so big, I wish she'd do something to hide it."

"Beatrice," I exclaimed, "you're still back in the age of the boyish form. Those breasts—they're not called bosoms anymore—breasts, Beatrice, breasts, they're her greatest assets. Believe me, I've seen the boys look at her and they weren't put off by her dirty feet. That girl, in bed, must be a movable feast."

Beatrice, I must say, didn't look particularly cheerful over this compliment to her granddaughter. So I went on, "In our day, our grandmothers, also our mothers, worried about virginity. Today you only worry about whether a sheep is a virgin."

"What do you mean, about sheep?"

"Virgin wool, you know."

She laughed. "Half the time, I never know when you're kidding, or not."

"Believe me, Beatrice, half the time I don't know myself."

Beatrice does a lot of loud sighing. "She's sloppy, I know. Looks dirty. But one thing you got to hand it to her. Her nails are always clean."

"How come?"

"Because she's a great reader."

"So?"

"All the time she cleans her nails on the corners of the pages."

"Your Rosemary," I say, "looks so tired and worn, maybe she ought to stay *out* of bed for a week or two."

Beatrice gives me the kind of look a grandchild gives you when you give him carrots.

"How long you think this religion thing's going to last?" I wonder.

When you get to an age at which you know more dead people than alive, you're bound to have learned something. And one thing is consoling, and that is that everything is temporary.

"I don't know, but as long as it's going on, I only hope," says Beatrice, "that Rosemary remembers to take her pill every morning. But for her, she says, it's not so important to use any contraceptives. No one worries anymore about whether a mother is married or not."

"Yes," I say, "I know, we're very old-fashioned. We like to have someone support the child. It's not nice to be practical. Too materialistic."

"Besides," she says, "nobody even cares anymore who the father is. And if she doesn't want to keep the baby, there's always some commune she can leave it at. Still"—Beatrice sighs—"I only hope she doesn't get caught."

"In our day," I remember, "we could do everything *but*. Save the cherry was like a slogan. They should have put it on billboards. Not that it was ever put that way."

"Reminds me," says Beatrice, "of that old 'knock-knock.'"

"Which one?"

"Knock, knock.

"Who's there?

"Hildegarde.

"Hildegarde who?

"Hildegarde the cherry, the fleet's in town."

"Believe me, we were born too early. What's so good about virginity, anyhow?"

"You're envying our granddaughters?"

"Yes, in a way, I am," I admitted. "Do you remember Celia Katz? She arranged her wedding night so she'd have the curse. That got her through."

"I often wondered how she worked it."

"Then there was another girl I knew. Shirley Geller. I don't think you knew her. She went to a doctor and had him put a few stitches in her you-know-what. When he finished, he said to her, 'Now I've restored your pristine virginity.' Her wedding night was a big success. For the man, I mean. Boy, did she have pains, like nobody's business."

"And now I worry only that Rosemary shouldn't get caught."

This is a problem, very familiar, from way back. Only we never called it religion.

Rosemary must be *very* tired. She wears a T-shirt says all across the front, "Phuque Off." These modern kids never did learn how to spell.

26

The Changing of the Will

The Changing of the Will, not like the Changing of the Guards, doesn't have to happen every day.

When you are angry at your children, wait a few days. Maybe they forgot to give you a purse or a slip for your birthday. Or maybe you phoned and your daughter-in-law answered and said your son was just watching television and couldn't come to the phone, or they were just leaving and couldn't talk, or maybe you were talking to him and she called him away to look at the roast because she was in the bathtub.

From television, your daughter or your daughters-in-law learn many things, like what perfume to buy; but about soaps and detergents to use in a hurry on the sink or the glassware when the mother-in-law's coming, this they turn off.

Then announce out loud, with plenty of noise, that you are leaving everything to the grandchildren. In trust, so nobody can touch it.

If the Agha Khan could do it, so can you. If the Emperor of Ethiopia could cut his eldest son out of his will, so can you.

You may not have an empire to fling around, but in your own way, you, too, can be a Maharani.

Churchill may have died in his nineties, but who knows but what he wasn't killed off by troubles with his children? Roosevelt, too. Does it pay to have children? Does it pay to have money?

If you have several sets of grandchildren, this business of will-changing will be more exciting, more disturbing, more aggravating for the parents of your darlings. Each set will speculate on how the other is doing.

Besides the money, you can spend many happy hours shifting around the silverware and the jewelry. Even if you don't use it, like a dozen oyster forks, don't give it to them now. Wrap it up, put it in the closet, on the top shelf; it isn't asking to be fed. Those oyster forks, by the way, I got from a cousin. Wonder who stuck her with them? Sometimes these gifts go the rounds for years, maybe getting back to the one who bought them or won them in a raffle in the first place.

Secretly, you are suspicious. You think maybe the children don't give a damn about your mother's heavy, fancy table settings anyhow. Only stainless steel they like. And the jewelry. What they can't sell, they will probably give it to the maid anyhow. Not that you can call her a maid anymore. *This* month she's a house-keeper.

"Next year," says Winthrop, "they'll call them house-hold science coordinators, and it'll cost another fifteen dollars a week."

When I was young, if you said "maid," you were put-ting on airs, *pish posh*. My mother said "hired girl" and when you said "right off the boat," you didn't mean bootlegging liquor, either. You meant that your father actually went down to the docks and picked out a Pol-ish girl for $12 a month. My father always picked the best-looking.

The mink coat, your teen-age granddaughter wouldn't wear, or even let her mother wear, because she's full of ecology.

Once when Arlene complained I shouldn't wear my mink coat what it took Harry thirty years before he bought me, I got a little annoyed.

"So how come you wear a leather-and-suede coat?" I asked her. "And shoes?" I was getting ungrand-motherly for a change.

"Oh," she comes right back, "it's O.K. These animals

weren't killed for their fur. Only for meat." She's not a vegetarian. Not yet, anyhow.

"We must preserve endangered species," she instructs me.

"So let the whooping cough cranes and the whales and the alligators watch out to preserve *me*," I answer. "I'm not getting any younger. I'm kind of endangered, too."

"But, Grandma, you're not really old," Arlene kisses me. "You're very well preserved."

"So what am I? Strawberry jam or a mummy?"

Every time I'm in the middle of some big family trouble—who's speaking to what, when, how, the telephone ringing, full of complaints, and everybody blaming somebody, mostly me, I shoulda said this, I shouldna done that, then in the mail comes lots of folders and letters all excited, I should save the bald eagles.

So never mind the mink coat in the will. Don't save it. Wear it to the supermarket even when you're carrying something leaky like cole slaw.

But when you want to buy something big, something you got to discuss with a husband, who objects, naturally, you say, "I should save the money for our daughters-in-law? They should spend it all in one week with the lavender boxes from Bergdorf's and the shopping bags from Bloomingdale's?"

Like Avis, I try harder. I mean I try to be just as extravagant as my daughters-in-law. When I buy something real expensive, maybe Harry says, "For God's sakes, we have to put aside something for our old age."

"Harry, my darling"—I look him straight in the eye—"this *is* our old age."

All the tshatchkes they don't want either. Unless you'll live long enough, then they'd be antiques and could be sold. Only money they accept, even for birthdays. You ask what they want, only one answer. One birthday, I remember, I said I'd give Jason a guitar I knew he wanted. So Cynthia says, "Better give him the money." I suppose there was something she wanted for the house.

Once, good and mad, I fixed my daughter-in-law, Melanie, but good. I sent twenty-five dollars to the cancer fund in her name. She got a card from them for her birthday present.

When changing the will, don't try saving on a lawyer, even though you're ashamed to face him too often. You may end up like Mrs. Regenbleit who died leaving seven handwritten wills, and everything going to the whereases.

And then there was my old friend, a widow, Julia Simons. No children, just dozens of nieces and nephews and grandnieces and grandnephews. Each one was supposed to get one hundred dollars flat for remembrance. Except the good ones that always sent birthday, Christmas and Chanukah cards. These got four hundred. But every time there was a fight, she changed things. Sometimes the four hundreds dropped to one, sometimes the ones dropped to nothing.

One niece, just for one Valentine card on which she signed her name (her mother spit on the stamp, Mr. Hallmark wrote the crap about how she loved a wonderful aunt), for this she was raised three hundred dollars.

When she died, everything was a mess. One niece she hadn't spoken to in three years because the smart-aleck, age fifteen, once told her aunt, "You're repressed sexually. You don't even know the difference between a vaginal orgasm and a clitoral one." True, she didn't know the difference. But who does? And who cares, anyhow? Just enjoy, enjoy. This niece, a four-hundred-dollar one, she forgot to leave out. But a darling little three-year-old she adored—he wasn't old enough yet to insult her—she forgot to mention. The lawyer was a nephew, but with all the changing going on, she forgot he was related and he was too polite to remind her. After any quarrel, if they made up, Julia'd sigh, "Sure, I made up with her, but it's costing me one hundred dollars."

One story about wills, let me tell you about my cousin, Reba. This cousin is a widow, without children, the biggest pain in the neck in the whole family. She went to my son Jason, the lawyer, and what happened?

Reba: I want to make out my will.

Jason: Good. You have brothers and sisters, about ten or eleven, I can't remember.

Reba: Nine living. *Momsers* every one of them.

Jason: Well let's get down to what you want to leave each one.

Reba: I wouldn't leave one lousy nickel to any of them. *Dreck,* the whole lot of them. Never invite me even to have a cup of coffee.

Jason: So, you'll leave everything to your nieces and nephews?

Reba: Never! The way those kids were brought up. They're horrible brats, no manners, no feelings, nothing. Not a red cent.

Jason: Cousins, then? Friends?

Reba: Cousins, troublemakers, all of them. And friends? Got rid of every last one of them. Not to be trusted. Two-faced *yentas.*

Jason: Well, then I suppose there's nothing left but to leave all your money to some favorite charity.

Reba screams: Charity? I worked hard all my life. Slaved in offices. Took dirt from bosses. And I should leave my hard-earned money, my life savings, to people I don't even know? You must be crazy.

Jason: Then what do you want to do?
Reba: That's what I came to you to find out.
Jason: I don't know what to suggest.
Reba gets up to go and yells: You're one hell of a lousy lawyer.

Don't hesitate to change your will three or four times a year. This gets plenty of people upset, and besides, you can enjoy your own death twenty years in advance. After each change, get out and treat yourself to a taxi. And announce out loud, "Let my heirs take the bus."

27
Your Grandson's Wedding

So, when you tell people your grandson is getting married and they ask, "What's the girl's ethnic background?" what it means, plain and simple, "Is he marrying a Jewish girl?"

If she's Jewish, you're just lucky it's not a mixed marriage. It used to be a mixed marriage was between two Jews, a *Galiciana* and a *Litvak*.

For wedding or bar mitzvah invitations, you remember some old arguments. No! I never hold a grudge even against some of those yentas who did things I'll never forgive.

You ask, maybe, what to give for a wedding present. They tell you, go see Mr. Tiffany. They're registered.

Maybe fingerprinted, too. Orders they left with him. He knows what they want. He knows how much you should spend, too.

At the wedding, don't forget for a minute that you are one of the most important persons there. The bride may have other ideas.

Before you sit down for the ceremony, they ask you which side you're from. Like it's a prizefight.

You expect the bride's mother to cry. What's to cry about? It took them twenty-five years to unload her, even if they say she's only twenty-two.

The bride's mother looks you straight in the eye and says, "I wasn't in a hurry for her to marry. I never worried."

Oh no! She never worried. She was only frantic.

Not that the bride isn't a fine girl. But how can you get enthusiastic about a girl from the Bronx? But who's a snob? No, I'm democratic. I believe in mixing, even from Brooklyn.

Since when do people from the Bronx have to be so refined they don't give you enough to eat? After the wedding, great-aunt Sophie complained she had to go to a cafeteria.

And they needn't have played a waltz for us elder statesmen. We can do modern dances—the fox-trot and the one-step. What do they think we are? The Moxie generation? At least we're not afraid to hold each other, not like these youngsters jumping up and down like they have St. Vitus dance, but four feet apart.

And Aunt Mamie they didn't invite. But the maid from the bride's family—her they had. The maid, they bragged, had been with them twenty years. Aunt Mamie's been with us longer.

But who's criticizing?

So one marries up, one marries down, you still have a seesaw, you still try to balance. Like one went to college, the other has the good looks. One comes from a better family, the other has money. Sometimes you stay on a seesaw, sometimes you fall off.

Her parents are sending the bridegroom, my grandson, through graduate school; they're buying him a house in Scarsdale, with a fancy decorator to tell him what kind of furniture he likes. A Mercedes-Benz they already bought him for the engagement, and now a honeymoon in Japan. But no dowry. That's un-American. You give a dowry, you might get into trouble with the Civil Liberties Union.

28

It's Chic to Be a Grandmother

Some of the best people are grandmothers, like Marlene Dietrich and Joan Bennett and Elizabeth Taylor. It's chic to be a grandmother, not sheik like in Rudolph Valentino, but chic like in classy Jackie Onassis. A grandmother is chic when she wears a *sheitel*, a wig.

Once, a woman at a canasta party, kept looking and looking at me. Finally, she couldn't stand it any longer, so she compliments me.

"You have so much hair. It must keep you warm."

Of course, she was dying to know if it was a wig and if there was tattletale gray underneath.

The old orthodox Jewish women had to cut off their hair when they married, like nuns marrying Jesus. This was so they wouldn't be attractive to other men. Now we wear wigs for the opposite reason.

Some, not so refined. "Is that your own hair?" they ask.

"Of course it's my own. I plunked down ninety good dollars for it."

It used to be, a woman was hot and tired, she went home and took off her girdle. Nowadays, she can hardly wait to peel off her hair and her eyelashes. Grandmothers look stylish these days, not like *alta bubbas*. You're slim, gaily dressed, and have all sorts of colored hair. Clairol blonde, moonglow, supersonic purple. Time was, not so long ago either, when you asked, "Does she or doesn't she?" it wasn't about hair dyes.

Contact lenses; eyelashes like awnings. Green paste on the lids. Lipstick put on with a paintbrush, to match the nail polish, with such names—Pink Poodle, Nearly Nude, Tomato Splash.

When the granddaughters get to be twelve, thirteen years old, the "borrowing" begins. They like your scarves, from Paris, your jewelry from Afghanistan, your fur-lined gloves from Spain, your sweaters from Scotland. If you should be mean enough to ask for something to come back (just to train them!), it will be found, maybe, next week. One violet-colored, real silk scarf from Hong Kong went back and forth between me and Arlene so many times that we lost track of who owned it. Who do you think has it now? I'll have to go back to Hong Kong for another one.

Of course, I'm tickled pink. You should have seen what *my* grandmother wore—except for tiny buttons of diamond earrings, even her own generation wouldn't have borrowed it.

But you can't be the younger set all the time, even though your granddaughter wants you to wear jeans.

So one day Jessica, age seven, I thought she was asleep on the folding cot in my room, watched me take out my dental bridge.

"Grandma," she speaks up, "you have a tunnel in your mouth?"

"How do you figure that, darling?"

"Well, I heard about dental bridges, but when we drive with Daddy, someone always asks should we take the tunnel or the bridge."

"Yes, dear? So?"

"Well, this didn't look anything like a bridge."

So after this, you don't count on children being deaf, dumb and blind. We weren't, with our parents, and what we heard and saw, and they never knew, was nobody's business. Only today's parents wouldn't bat an eyelash. They'd call it educational. It was educational for us, too. Only more so. So, undress in the bathroom even if the child seems to be sleeping like a log. What this means, I'm not sure. I never saw a log sleep.

You read enough, and follow instructions of *Vogue* and *Glamour* and *Girl Talk* at the beauty parlor, you can brag that everybody in the supermarket and in the playground mistakes you for the children's mother. Only don't mention *Girl Talk* to the women libbers in your family. A long, hysterical lecture you'll get on how women are insulted by being called girls. I should be so insulted.

Also, if you live long enough, you hear everything. Nowadays you mustn't use Webster's dictionary. Mr. Noah gave insulting definitions to women. Women's Lib doesn't like him. Only now, maybe starting last week, I think you can't say Women's Lib anymore. They're Feminists.

And don't look surprised when your eight-year-old granddaughter (her mother, she runs to meetings, carries signs, and takes courses in "self-assertiveness," as though she needs more of it) suddenly asks, "Grandma, do you still menstruate?"

What she also wanted to ask is if Grandpa Harry and I still—you know what. If she'd ask, I'd have told her that practice makes perfect. Can I tell her, two, three times a week, for forty years, I've been losing my virginity? The kids think my whole generation is backward. Some look it. Even when they have children, they look and act so stifflike, it seems they forgot how they got started.

But not the widows. Me, I have a husband, thank the Lord Old Mighty. But many of my friends, also grandmothers, are widows. And sometimes they get courted by widowers. The men are about the same age, but the women, suddenly they're ten years younger. But who's counting? All of us, the friends, have to be ten years younger, too—and do they have problems! To keep secret:

False teeth
Wigs, all colors
Dyed hair. If you see gray, it's because she's allergic to dye.
False eyelashes
Contact lenses
Fanny hikers
Tiredness
Stomachaches
Backaches
Constipation
Support hose

Hearing aides hiding in eyeglasses
Varicose veins
Droopy breasts, nicely held up with wires
Droopy fannies likewise I'm sure
And a hair on the chin. God forbid they should cut it with scissors. No they run to a specialist to have it electrocuted.

But one thing they've still got. And that's good, healthy sex feelings. Even in the old-age homes, there's plenty hanky-panky going on, and in the afternoons, the French way.

The courtship, though, has to be the restrained kind of a type. The gentleman makes advances. He does research. He knows you're no spring chicken, but a hunk of cold steer liver in bed he doesn't want. A centerfold for *Playboy*, maybe she was, thirty years ago, but now, the lady is not. So if she's lucky, he's full of old-fashioned respect for womanhood.

These gentlemen are often brought back from those tours, "For Singles over Thirty-five." If one woman under sixty is on the tour, she gets the one man. You wonder if he even paid for the trip. Maybe he's hired by the travel agency. A shill, it's called.

Most of the time these bachelors or widowers don't even have intentions to marry. Half blind he can be, a little lame, he still gets invited to parties, to dinners, all the widows and divorcées dangling in front of him like a yoyo. When he was young, maybe he had pimples, was short, the girls wouldn't give him the time of day. He never made time with anyone. Now he's important. Why should he change anything? He never had it so good.

And the trouble they have keeping hidden the older grandchildren. Only the very youngest ones are brought out and shown off. Even the photographs of the older grandchildren have to be hidden away when the gentleman caller comes around.

Nowadays, you're never the older generation, or elderly, you're very classy as senior citizens. But if you're collecting social security, you don't tell the suitor. And from one of the granddaughters, my Jessica, this question comes.

"Grandma, when you get on a bus with your friends, do you use your senior discount pass?"

This depends on which friend it is. Also, if she happens to have an unmarried escort along.

And at the movies. The lady has to stand there, all innocent-like, while the gentleman caller buys the tickets. Like she's too young to have ever heard about Golden Age Discount Cards, right there in her purse.

Once, my friend Sadie brought around a nice, good-looking prospect, very serious, with an income, for all the "girls" to inspect. This made all the husbands very irritable.

Another time, Ella produced something, a specimen of a man who looked three days dead. On a desert island you wouldn't give him a tumble. This made the husbands very happy. "See what you'd get if you killed me off," says my Harry, full of bounce, the momser.

One friend, Stella, got herself a very nice second husband. When she married, no birth certificate around anyhow, she made a mistake about her age on her passport. She was ten years younger than on her old passport, the one she tore up. Then comes invitations to class reunions, bring husband. Naturally, she can't go.

"I don't want Michael to see all these old women. Besides, maybe he thinks I'm smart, but smart enough to graduate high school at the age of *eight?*"

And then there's Bertha. She lopped off so many years from her age when she married, that she had to pretend she was still menstruating every month. Wore old-fashioned Kotex pads to prove it. When she was young enough to menstruate, they hadn't even invented Tampax yet.

When you've still got a senior-citizen husband you're lucky even if there were times in the past you didn't think so. He may not be as tall as Mount Everest but thank God he's there.

After forty-five years you and your husband don't bother to look at each other with a sharp eye. And you've also stopped trying to understand each other. That's good, because too much understanding can ruin a marriage. You're just glad to feel you're both there. Some people, very quick on figures, count how much the food costs at the supermarket before they get to the cashier. They can count things about the stock market and they can count how many hours the grandchildren spent on television and shouldn't. But there's one thing you can't count even on a computer—and that's your blessings.

You can concentrate on being a grandmother. One day, I remember, I was concentrating so much, playing with three little ones, me sprawled right on the living-room floor, that my son Winthrop, the doctor, says about me, to no one in particular: "What a pity. She would have made an excellent mother."

My friend Frieda Eisenstein says, "They say every mother should start with the third child. You know what? Every mother should start as a grandmother."

A Jewish Grandmother. But, what with ancestor worship, it's better to be Chinese. Maybe *besser*, a Jewish-Chinese?

Everybody loves his Jewish Grandmother. Why? Who knows? But you must be doing something right, at last.

29

Grandmother's Day

A Grandmother's Day, there is no such thing. We should picket the greeting-card manufacturers.

The signs should read: "*Bubba* loves you. But who loves *Bubba?*"

Greeting cards—with tinsel, with jewels, with perfume, with folding flowers that hit you in the face with God knows what—they have for Mr. Washington's birthday, for Mr. Lincoln, for Mr. Valentine, for Mr. Halloween, for Mr. Columbus. All men, mind you. Mothers are thrown in just for what they call a token. (Not the kind you use on the subway.) For hurricanes, so far, they have only female names. But for grandmothers, no special day.

On TV, a beautiful model squeezes the toilet paper, pets it, smirks at it, fondles it. Toilet paper, I sometimes think, gets more love than a grandmother.

After all, there's a Mother's Day, and maybe "Mother" is a dirty word to Mr. Freud, but not Grandmother. Not yet, anyhow.

On Mother's Day, from my grandson, he should live and be well, I get a bottle of Arpège. Over forty years Harry and I've been married and, believe me, he never promised me anything. But still, now I have a bottle of Arpège. From a grandson, yet.

Now here's one grandmother that's going to smell as good as a plate of fresh chicken soup.

"You don't douse yourself with such expensive perfume," warns my daughter, Elana. "It's not toilet water. You just put a drop behind each earlobe."

"Not me! I'll put it in *front* of the earlobe."

Now, when I'm all dressed up and smelling like a hothouse, often I'll lean over Harry and say, "Smell my earlobes."

"What some people won't do," he grabs me, "to get an extra kiss."

For Mother's Day, my daughter-in-law gives me a shocking-pink nylon waltz gown. After the late-late show, so late it's the early-early show, I get ready for bed. So who's waltzing?

My daughter Elana, the literary one, she sees her

husband working on income tax and says, "'April is the cruelest month.'"

She's wrong. So wrong. The cruelest month is May when comes Mother's Day. From some of the children, no presents, not even cards. They don't know yet Don Ameche invented the telephone. Or maybe a gift from the corner drugstore where they don't exchange. Sometimes I hate the woman who thought up Mother's Day.

Time was, they used to say, if a boy is good to his mother, he'll be a good husband. No more. Now, if a boy loves his mother, he has to go to a psychiatrist. He learns how to pretend she doesn't exist on Mother's Day. This costs fifty dollars an hour. A mother can still love a son. This doesn't cost anything.

Then later, if he starts remembering your birthday and gets polite once in a blue moon and asks how you are and asks you over for dinner, when he has friends there, then's the time to worry. It means he doesn't love you anymore.

Sometimes you feel down, you figure the only reward you can count on will come in heaven. And not a minute sooner.

Nowadays, there are pills for everything. To put you to sleep, to wake you up, to make you forget something, to make you remember, God knows what. What we really need is only one thing—a one-a-day feel-loved pill.

But everything cheers up when a grandchild remembers. Especially if the little darling makes something herself with crayons and paste and knitting wool, all drippy and bunched up. With maybe a gumdrop stuck on it. A Picasso it's not. But Picasso, I don't always like either. When a grandchild draws a picture, a woman has only two eyes. With Picasso, you never know. What man is looking for a woman with three eyes? Three breasts, maybe, but not three eyes, and a clock in the head.

Mother's Day, I can do without. You go to restaurants and you see that all the old-age homes emptied for the afternoon. Other family groups, children, grandchildren, big crowd all together, not everyone on friendly terms other days; they eat together now, and Father or Mother pays the check. You'd like all the children and grandchildren together, eating, shouting, pushing. But no! One set of Jewish princesses doesn't want to eat with the mother of one of the Jewish princes. This day, royalty isn't speaking.

"What's the quarrel about?" you ask.

"It has something to do," says Jason, "with the Chancellor of the Exchequer."

"Translated from British to English," says Harry, "this means there was a fight about money."

Maybe children never really grow up until both parents are dead, even if the parents live to be ninety.

Sometimes, when one of my children is acting badly, very badly, I wish I was dead so they'd grow up and be nicer to me.

Maybe our attitude is all wrong, right from the beginning. We should feel that our children weren't *given* to us, only lent. We can enjoy loving them, and that's all we're entitled to.

Grandmother's Day, that would be different. It should be a national holiday, with parades and floats on Fifth Avenue and the grandmothers waving and smiling from the line of cars all hung with confetti. And TV cameras asking you to smile and give your name and how many beautiful grandchildren you got. And all the friends and relatives hanging on the six o'clock news to see your face, like you're getting an Oscar or, more appropriately, a Grammy.

30

The Subject Is Noses

Any nose, as long as it's not like that man's, Cyrano's, is all right on a Gentile, or even on an Arab, those other Semites. But on a Jewish girl, a nose has to be short, straight, and turn up a little. In America, that is. You look at French movies, or Italian, and the beautiful heroines all the men get hot for don't have teeny, weensie buttons for noses. You travel in Turkey, all the noses are enormous. Born in Turkey, I'd have been a raving beauty.

My granddaughter Jessica, sixteen years old and a beauty, believe me, has big dark eyes like black jumbo olives, black hair that comes down her back like a curtain to the top of her faded jeans, and hardly a pimple since her mother took her to a skin doctor. Besides, she has legs so long, they come all the way up from the ground to make four very nice bulges, two in back and two higher up in front.

"What do you want for your coming-out party?" I asked, and she answered very quickly, "A new nose."

"She feels insecure," her mother explained.

And who doesn't? My own nose, not very big, but not one I adore when looking in the mirror to powder it, never gave me great joy either. I used to see, when I was young, Gentile girls with terrible troubles, about lovers, family, or jobs, and wonder how girls with such beautiful, small, cute noses could have any problems at all.

Now you take my grandmother from Poland. She had Negroid features—thick lips, a broad nose. From what kind of a pogrom did this come? Pushkin, maybe? The other pogroms bring out looks more like Cossacks or Tartars; to some people those pogroms now seem sort of kindly, like benefits.

Even before I agreed, Jessica explained, "I have the doctor all picked out. He did a swell job on my friend Pam." She paused. "She has a new boyfriend. A dream!"

I didn't have to worry about Harry. For a granddaughter, if she asked him to get the Mafia to murder a girl friend she had a fight with, it'd be O.K. with him.

As a matter of fact, when the children are at my house and Harry urges, "Have a little more chicken, darling" or "Never mind your diet, take another piece of Grandma's strudel, made from scratch," our Jessica laughs, "Grandpa Harry, you're more of a Jewish grandma than Grandma is."

So we went to consult Dr. Saltpeter. What went on in that waiting room should be on a TV program. It's not like other doctors' offices where no one speaks or even looks at you except maybe to say, "Would you mind passing that *New Yorker* magazine?" Here everybody talked. They talked about everything except how much they paid. Sample conversations:

"My cousin's nose came out swell. So what happens? Someone gets the idea to tell her it took all the character out of her face."

"My boyfriend, he didn't want me to have it done. Said I looked like a painting by Raphael or Titian. But me, I want to look American."

Most of the patients had noses all bandaged up in pink. One woman's face was open, but her breasts looked enormous. Probably bandaged. Reminded me of my friend Mildred, who had her breasts made *smaller,* mind you, not bigger, when she got a divorce after thirty years of marriage. When she was a girl, breasts were supposed to be small. You flattened them down with boyish-form brassieres. Hers were large and hanging. She was always self-conscious. Later, when breasts were supposed to be big, even if you had to stuff them up with padding or silicone, she still couldn't feel stylish. So she had them reduced and shaped. The doctor said he never did that before to a woman her age. Now, when she has lunch with you in a restaurant, she takes you into the ladies' room, takes off her blouse and brassiere, and shows off her new, expensive breasts. They look like the bumps just beginning to develop on a young girl who's worried stiff they may not get big enough.

In the waiting room there was one man with ears all bandaged with adhesive. Looked like pink earmuffs. He was inspecting a pair of bookends on the table in front of him. The bookends were bronzed, like baby's first shoes. One was a large humped nose (the "before"), and the other was a dainty little gem (the "after").

The conversation goes on:

"My father tried to stop me. He says when you have cancer, it's time enough for an operation."

I looked around. Everybody looked as though they'd been in barroom fights, especially one man, with his mouth all kind of black and blue and twisted.

A woman announced: "Dr. Saltpeter grafted skin on my cheek over a burn. The matching of skin," she explained, "is done like weaving. The grain of the skin has to be followed. *My* defect," she spoke, so hoity-toity, "was not one I was *born* with."

All sorts of confidences came out:

"I took up skiing in the hope that I'd fall on my nose and be forced to have a plastic." She laughed. "We skied so much my husband broke his leg."

By this time, Jessica and I were having such a ball, we almost forgot what we came for. No hurry. We still had hours before the doctor would get to us. But Jessica was losing her nervousness.

"Dr. Saltpeter told me he doesn't like a *small* nose. He praised me for having a big one. Said he likes plenty of material to work with."

"With me, he kept a running commentary all through the operation. That's the advantage, or maybe disadvantage, of having a local anesthetic. As he wielded that scalpel, he'd gloat, 'Well, there goes the bulge at the tip, here goes the last of the lump.' He sounded so joyful. Made me almost sorry to lose a lifelong accessory."

"How long," someone asked, "before you get rid of all the bandages?"

"Depends on the rate of healing. I'm due for an unveiling next visit, I hope."

Suddenly from the other room, came a cry.

"That sounded like a baby."

"I coulda sworn it was a baby."

"My husband was nice about my plastic. Says I shouldn't mind walking around with the bandages on because everybody recognizes a plastic. It's an expensive operation. Shows your husband is doing well."

The expensive part, I heard. This is what they call the "operative" word and it has nothing to do with the operation.

"I couldn't go to the PTA meeting the other night. They would have withdrawn my son's scholarship. They gave it on the basis of need."

"The trouble with my family, they keep telling me about my cousin Lottie," said another. "She has a big nose and she married a doctor. Not good-looking, though. A shrimp. Nothing like Dr. Saltpeter."

Sudden silence. Everyone thinking of the handsome doctor. Everyone was in love with him for a few minutes. It was quiet, like a memorial service.

"Still," someone broke the spell, "a doctor is a doctor."

And a nose is a nose is a nose.

Two women standing at the window were comparing snapshots. "This is how I looked before. You can see my nose wasn't long at all."

"Neither was mine. Everybody said I was crazy. But I had it done mostly because of a deviated septum."

Later, after the operation, I found out about all those snapshots they showed. The faces were so tiny you couldn't tell the nose from a hole in the wall. And so many deviated septums were reported, you'd be surprised.

One girl, looking into her compact mirror, said, "Believe me, I got a good mind to take off the bandage and get a peek at it."

Everybody stopped talking and egged her on. "Go on, take it off. You can paste it back on. The doctor'll never know."

She slipped it off.

"Gorgeous."

"Beautiful."

Her girl friend shrieked. "Sadie, it's wonderful. You look just like a shiksa."

Now, I could guess, her name won't be Sadie very long.

Then there came out from the other room, something that made everyone stop talking. Suddenly, it was so quiet, a schoolteacher would have been proud of her class. An English nurse, in a uniform, with a long blue veil fluttering from her head, was carrying an infant in her arms. A mother, all flustered, in a mink coat, followed. At the exit door stood a chauffeur in uniform; he was carrying an oilskin diaper bag. The mother held a plastic baby bottle. They all swept out like the end of a second act.

Hubbub! "They're certainly having noses done at an early age these days."

The receptionist finally spoke. "Harelip," she explained.

"Oh." Everyone sighed with relief.

"The baby was born with a hole in the center of her face," the receptionist went on. "You should have seen her. She looked like a little pig."

Then the receptionist told Jessica and me to go into the office. Jessica, scared a little, and I, deciding that whatever the charges, it'll be O.K. with me and certainly with Grandpa Harry.

And now I'm ashamed to tell you what happened in that office. We came out with an appointment for a week from Tuesday, at Mount Sinai Hospital. But it wasn't for one operation. It was for two! And who else was going to have a nose job? You guessed it.

Jessica's idea, of course. "I have never thought of it, Grandma, until we were sitting in that office and Dr. Saltpeter was drawing pictures of noses and asking me which one I liked."

When she asked my opinion, and I picked out a nice Elizabeth Taylor type, she turned to me and said, "Grandma, this would look just gorgeous on you. Elizabeth Taylor is a grandmother, too."

That did it. I was afraid to go home and tell Harry. But my Harry is a doll, a living doll. He only laughed.

"Maybe you'll get on TV. Granddaughter and grandmother have twin noses. Maybe on the 'Today' show. Or an interview with Barbara Walters. She'll show how Women's Lib lets grandmothers express themselves. Not," he added, "that you were ever shy in that department."

"So everything's coming up noses."

Just before the operation, Jessica pulled out another trick. Full of smiles, she says to the handsome doctor, "While I'm on the table, Dr. Saltpeter, would you do me one tiny, little favor?"

"What is it?"

"Just, please, pierce my ears for me."

The doctor laughed. "It's not the first request of that nature. For *you*, my dear, yes, I'll pierce them." Sounded to me like bargaining in the Casbah, especially when he added, "At no extra charge."

"Thank you," she says sweetly. "Only one hole in each ear."

"How many would anyone want?" he asks.

"Oh, lots of the kids are having two and three holes. They'll wear loops and studs and stars and pendants all at once. It's the latest thing."

The following week, we walked out of that hospital together, Jessica and I. All bandaged, eyes black and blue, Gentile bandages, Gentile black eyes. When Fanny Brice, years ago, had her nose bobbed, the popular wisecrack was, "She cut off her nose to spite her race."

Some people go into a hospital to change their sex. We went in to change what they call, so politely, our ethnic background. Now we were two shiksas who still wanted to be Jews, but not to look it.

Jessica's nose came out of hiding a perfect jewel. She wears out all the mirrors in the house, admiring herself. Front face, profile, left, right, backward, forward. She could stand on her head and it would look perfect. Her friends are busy with their Kodak Instamatics. She pays for the films and the developing. One of her boyfriends wrote her a note saying her nose was "tip-tilted like the petal of a rose."

"He got that out of Bartlett's Quotations," says Jessica, but she was full of glow, like she had a Sabbath candle burning inside. This new boyfriend—an older man. Eighteen!

And her disposition. So sweet, all the time. Before, she was going through what they called a "phase." But you weren't supposed to worry, you weren't allowed to scold, it was supposed to be normal. When someone said, "Have a nice day," you were afraid she'd snap, "Don't tell me what to do."

When she used to cross a street, and the sign said, "Walk," or "Don't walk," she'd get angry. "Takes away my choice of independent action," she'd explain.

"Pass the salt," you might ask.

"Don't give me orders."

Now, all of a sudden, she's so obliging and polite, it's positively frightening. God willing, it's just another phase and won't last. Now, sometimes, her smile is so sweet it's lucky I'm not diabetic.

Another change is the clothes she wears. Now she dresses to look like a girl. Before, with those unisex clothes, she was one of those you'd see walking down the street, usually in bunches, and you couldn't tell which were boys and which were girls. When I mentioned this once, Jessica instructed me, "You can look—you know—in the place—you know—where it shows—I mean where the crotch is."

Harry pretended to look surprised. "Oh," he asked, "do they still have *that* difference?"

Now her clothes vary, but always like a girl. She wears jeans, she looks as though her behind had been boiled down to a liquid, poured in, and then solidified, like jello. Well solidified. When she flounces around in a bikini, she looks so natural, as though she didn't need any new clothes since she was in diapers.

"She'll always remember this time in her life," says Harry.

"Of course, and so will I."

"The days of wine and noses."

My nose? Not quite perfect, but improved. At least

it's a different nose, and not the one that gave me shivers when I was younger. Not the one uncles and cousins (their noses no smaller) used to make wise-cracks about, used to kid me. Kidding? I'd wind up in tears, but in private. Young girls were supposed to be good-natured all the time around men. Thank God today for Women's Lib. *Nobody* has to have a good disposition all the time. With their permission, you can be as unpleasant as you like, and it's not because you're a nasty person. It's for a cause.

But Women's Lib should give us credit. We Jews really go in for equal sex. The boys are circumcised where it counts and the girls are having their noses circumcised.

Not that I didn't have plenty of boyfriends when I was young, and they were full of compliments about my looks. Maybe I only got the ones with poor eyesight. Now, with a brand-new nose, I have a whole new set of reactions. Mine, not other people's.

Now that I'm on my way to scaring the life out of glamorous movie star grandmothers, I've decided to top it all off, like a blob of whipped cream, with a face lift.

When people start telling you "You look wonderful for your age," you know you look very old. "Well preserved" is another kind of insult.

I'll spring it on Harry when we're walking in Central

Park or on Riverside Drive. Why? Because there's no ceiling for him to hit.

My nose? Well, it's shorter, it's straighter; but Zsa Zsa Gabor, I'm not. Ingrid Bergman? Maybe. But you know what? I still look like a Jewish grandmother.

31

The Liberated Grandmother

Shira on the telephone, tears, real and exaggerated.

"Grandma, please come over and take me out for a pizza and a movie." She was choking on grief and a chocolate brownie. "Please, Grandma." Pause. "And a lottery ticket."

So I told Harry what's in the icebox for lunch. I wasn't worried about staying home and doing it for him. Since he's retired, I'm kind of a liberated woman myself. Not that he's like other men you can plop in front of TV for the sports. He's not interested. Whatever I suggest he should do for a hobby—golf, fishing, joining a chess club—he says, "It's funny. Whatever you want me to do seems to be something out of the house."

"How about all those things you always said you'd do after you retired?" I ask.

Harry laughs. "I can't remember what they were."

There ought to be a nursery school for retired husbands. Another thing that doesn't put him into a nice coma is one of those old TV movies where people kiss with all their clothes on.

"Just put the clothes in the washing machine," I told him. "They're all ready—in the kitchen."

"Someone should invent a machine that eats socks in *pairs* so you don't know they're missing," he suggested.

Since Harry's retired, there's one thing I miss most. No privacy for nice, long telephone conversations. If someone in the next room is listening, it's hard to talk. You have to be so *accurate*.

I put on my wig that matches my natural hair that I had dyed to match my wig. I got dressed up in my Mexican poncho that some granddaughter will tease me out of. Three times already, one of the girls admired it. Sure sign. It's too cold for me, anyhow; the wind blows up my armpits.

"Whoever heard of cold armpits?"

"Now you're hearing." I explained to Harry. "Something's wrong at Melanie's."

"You seem pretty happy about it." The momser!

My daughter-in-law, God bless her, is a very modern Women's libber. Sometimes she's up, sometimes she's down, like the stock Harry buys each grandchild when he's born—General Motors, American Kiss and Tell. Usually she's running around all over town like a chicken without a head. Is that an occupation for a Jewish girl? Cutting off the head is not even the kosher way to kill a chicken. When other people have moods, they get mad, they hate everybody all morning, then for lunch they make some bacon and eggs, slam the pots around, feel better and, if there's no school, take the kids out for the afternoon.

But not my daughter-in-law Melanie. *She* has an identity crisis. When Shira asked her to zip up the back of her blouse, Melanie yelled. "I will not, positively not, be relegated in life to the role of nursemaid. Go ask your father to attend to his children."

Whose children they are always depends on who's being annoyed with them. Owners of children, in all families, I notice, can change from hour to hour. It's lucky it doesn't have to be registered each time, like a car.

I notice that an identity crisis always comes the day the maid is off. On other days, Melanie isn't home because after all the children started school, she finished college and got a good part-time job. Now she's a psychology major, with a master's degree, and God knows what else if you can listen to her mother. Not that she wasn't tickled pink to marry a doctor. And such a handsome doctor, my son. He shouldn't be practicing medicine at all. He ought to be a doctor on one of those television shows about medicine.

My son is only, her mother says, an ophthalmologist. That's what we used to call an eye doctor so people knew what you were talking about. Even if you could learn to spell it, you'd never be able to pronounce it. You should hear her mother talk about the wonderful men Melanie could have married. All of them rich, from important families, such men as never even existed, if you ask me.

Now, says Melanie, all excited, red in the face, my son should work only part time and share the household responsibilities. So, who's going to pay for all the pantsuits from Bergdorf's? Other women look at Bergdorf's and buy at Ohrbach's. They figure, if you don't buy at an expensive store, you save more money than if you don't buy at a cheaper place. But not Melanie. She doesn't even know there are any stores farther downtown than Saks Fifth Avenue. If the saleslady doesn't have some kind of an accent and call her M'damn, she won't even try on a Bill Blass scarf. I wonder if they have some kind of a training course to get those accents. Without it, the saleslady would have to work at Ohrbach's.

Others have their nails manicured; not Melanie. She has hers "sculptured."

In my day we had bad moods, too. We didn't have a fancy name for it. We just said it was our period coming on. Or that we got up on the wrong side of the bed. No mix-up there. We *knew* whose bed we got up wrong from. If there was any hanky-panky, we didn't go talking about it all over town like it was some kind of group therapy. These new feminists think that to meet a man halfway you have to go all the way. We were confused, too, about many things, but not about *that*. Open marriage nowadays means you talk about it, you open up to everybody. When a child got on our nerves, maybe she got a whack she shouldn't have, but we didn't tell her we wished abortion had been legal when she was conceived. It would have been all right to tell her because an eleven-year-old in those days didn't know what an abortion was, anyhow. My own grandmother didn't know.

Just because you planned the child doesn't mean you'll get the kind of child you planned.

Melanie wailed, "I'm so frustrated. Marriage is so narrowing and confining for women."

"Well, who isn't frustrated?" I asked. "Men are, too."

"I don't know what to do." She slapped her forehead.

What to do about getting lunch, she doesn't know. But about transactional analysis she knows a lot. The first thing, she says, everyone should learn is "Know yourself." Some Greek guy said it. Not Onassis or Nick the Greek. Some old fellow, who drank something I never saw advertised, called hemlock.

Believe me, knowing myself is the last thing I want to do. With too much understanding, perhaps I wouldn't get along so well. It'd make me nervous. Everybody is looking for identity, as though it's something you can find in a department store or hiding in a closet. Me! I like to *lose* mine. That's why I go to the movies.

Melanie moaned, "I can't realize my potential as a complete human being. I'm not a total person."

Life is cruelly circumscribing her by thrusting her into a purely feminine role. My son, the children heard, is the victimizer.

"No country in the world, except America," she wailed, "expects a mother to have the exclusive company of children. No primitive society condones it."

"Your whole generation's conditioning," she said to me, "was stultifying. You were taught to lead lives of quiet desperation."

Annoyed, I answered, "that's good training. Because that's the kind of life most people lead. Some are quiet about it. Women's libbers are not so quiet. But desperate, yes, all of us."

She looked at my two darling grandchildren and groaned. Loud. So that my son in the next room would hear it.

"I lose my identity," she announced, as over a loudspeaker, "whenever I'm with a member of the family." Not much of a loss, if you ask me.

For a brilliant girl, believe me, Melanie is an awful dope. One trouble with Melanie is that she thinks people are supposed to be happy. Who's happy? Not even God, I bet. But I don't argue with her. With a daughter-in-law you have to be sincere, even if you don't mean it.

Everything bad that happens is supposed to be due to marriage, not exactly *her* marriage, but the institution and the terrible way women are treated.

"All my friends' marriages"—she glares at me as though everything, all of civilization, is my fault—"are deplorable." She sighs. "Husbands have to be rehumanized."

We used to be told that marriage was invented by women for their own protection. Now, it seems, marriage was invented by men just to insult women. Among my own friends, the attitude is different. As long as a marriage lasts, it's considered a good marriage.

At this point, and just what we needed, there arrived a visitor, a young woman, a friend of Melanie's. You could see by her face that she came with plenty of problems. She motioned to Melanie to go in the bedroom.

"That button she was wearing," said Shira, "what does it mean?"

"What did it say?" As though I didn't know.

"It said 'I am a Lesbian.' What's a Lesbian?"

I thought fast. "It's a kind of religion."

"Oh, like Catholic or Jewish?"

"Yes." I got very enthusiastic. I didn't exactly lie to her. The way some of these women's libbers, feminists, I mean, carry on, you'd think it was a new religion.

Just as she was leaving, she happened to mention that she has a daughter about Shira's age.

"How many children do you have?" Shira asked.

"I'm the ex-mother of three. But there'll be no more. Lesbianism is the purest form of contraception." She left, slamming the door.

"Grandma," asked Shira, "what's an ex-mother?"

"Oh," I explained (this was an easy one), "ex is short for excellent.

I'm certainly not against the feminists. I'm all for them, the best parts, I mean. If you're working on a job, which would you rather have, more pay or a few men that should jump up when you enter a room? Besides, how many actually jump up and from how many chairs?

Melanie explained to me later why this dame has to wear the button. "Every experience is a liberating force. Something to be proud of."

"I can think of plenty of experiences I'm not so proud of," I answered, "and some other ones I'd rather not be so liberated about. Like maybe 'I've been mugged' or 'I had cholera.'"

Nowadays, I'm learning a lot. For instance, you're not supposed to have a baby if you're married. You must adopt one, and the child has to be a different color. If you're *not* married, it's different. Then it's all right to have a baby.

And you mustn't be heterosexual, God forbid. That means a man only has sex with women and women with men. You have to be bisexual. When you get right down to it, either way it's just friction.

When you are going through an identity crisis, the whole world is out to belittle you. Even television. During the day, Melanie breaths freely, but on the six o'clock news she hears about the high-density fuel oils lousing up the air. The air is unacceptable. Is this because women are sex objects? What can you do with air that's unacceptable? You don't accept it, I suppose.

Something else for Melanie to reject. Perhaps, you return it? For credit?

Even the Bible, Melanie explained, is sexist. "The audacity of it," she wailed, "saying man cannot live by bread alone."

She's right. Women need bread, too, but not alone. With a nice piece of Muenster cheese.

I never knew she had so much education from the Bible. "What is man that thou art mindful of him? Women are omitted from everything spiritual."

"Now, I suppose," I said, "they'll be forming committees to take up with God that he should be mindful of women, too."

It was a crisis all day and all evening. For everybody. Another Watergate, only it was worse, because it was right in your own house.

But you know what? I have plenty of friends who wouldn't understand all the trouble. They'd give their right arm to be exploited as sex objects again.

32

Speaking of Operations–
This One You Don't

When your daughter-in-law Cynthia, who never asked your opinion on anything in all the years she's married, suddenly comes to you, all sweetness and light, to ask your advice, it means she wants you to do something you don't want to do.

"Jason," she said, "had a vasectomy."

"What's that?" you ask. I thought it was something illegal, like larceny or felony. He's the son that's a lawyer.

"It's an operation," she explained, "that cuts off the

sperm so he can't have any more children. Two's enough.

"So why couldn't you keep on with the Pill?"

"It nauseates me."

"Only since you read that book about the doctor's case against the Pill."

"Anyway this is the problem. Jason wears a pin in his lapel. It's the male symbol, a circle with an arrow sticking up, indecent if you ask me, with the arrow so stiff, and the circle is broken a little. Underneath it says 'vasectomy.'

"He says it's very stylish to wear it nowadays." Cynthia sighs.

So now we come to the problem. My daughter-in-law explains. "Wherever we go now, all the women swarm around him. He's the life of the party. And what's more, they have the audacity to ask me if it interferes with his virility."

"Does it?" I asked.

"That's not the point."

For me it's not the point. But for her?

So I laugh. I can't stop laughing. My daughter-in-law wants me to try and convince him not to wear the pin. Such a problem, my grandmother, may she rest in peace, with her nine children should have had.

I can't stop laughing.

"Other men," she goes on, "are starting to wear the pin, too."

"An organization?" I asked. "Like No-Sperm Anony-
mous."

She smiles, but not like she's happy. More like a
crack in the plaster on the wall above the kitchen sink.

"Talk to him, Mother."

All of a sudden I'm promoted to "Mother." In this
conversation my position rises every minute. In the
shake of a lamb's tail I'll be Queen of the May yet.
Ruth and Naomi, from the Bible, we are not. Though
my daughter-in-law sometimes stands on the corniest
ideas.

Now I draw myself up, very noble, like I had an
English nanny in my childhood.

"I'm the kind of a type that never interferes."

Show character.

So when I get Jason alone, I say to him, "This vasectomy thing. It's permanent?"

"Not necessarily. Some doctors say it's reversible."
He smiled. "Not that I care, you know."

"But, Jason, no more grandchildren from you? Only
all kinds of women sniffing around you?"

"Mother"—he laughed—"I wouldn't change it for the
world. I never had it so good."

But I'm not happy. God picked us grandmothers out
especially—Gentile, Hindu, Buddhist, Vegetarian,
Atheist, or whatever, even Republican—while still in
our mothers' wombs, to be Jewish Grandmothers.

Bibliography

Grandmothers are not a recent phenomenon. They have been prevalent in literature since the dawn of history. Everybody, except Cain and Abel, had them. Jewish grandmothers, all. Here is a list of source material.

Spinoza—His own Jewish grandmother was greatly distressed over his unorthodox opinions. He wouldn't wear a *yarmulka*.

Copernicus—He proved that the earth revolves around the sun. He didn't know that the whole world revolves around the grandchildren. His Polish mother knew.

Socrates—He not only had trouble with Xantippe, but also with his mother, who didn't like the way her grandchildren were running around barefoot in Athens.

Shakespeare—King Lear was a grandfather. Once he had a wife, who would have been a grandmother had she lived, *Olav hasholem*.

Oedipus—His wife was grandmother to her own children. This complicated matters.

Galileo—His children's grandmother kept telling him not to teach the little darlings such radical ideas. Finally when he was almost burned at the stake, he realized that grandmothers are always right.

Darwin—He also had a grandmother and she was not a monkey, as generally supposed. She convinced him that the theory of evolution means that the grandchildren should do better than the parents. This made her a Jewish grandmother.

Civilizations crumble, monuments disintegrate, nations perish, cultures are wiped out by conquering armies, mountains are corroded into the sea, but grandmothers go on forever.

Glossary

Bar Mitzvah—The thirteenth birthday. "Today I am a man" day. But a boy can still be ordered around, especially by a grandmother.

Besser—More better.

Bubba—Grandmother. Formerly a term of respect. *Alta bubba* is a grandmother who doesn't go to the beauty parlor.

Chanukah—Jewish Christmas. With presents; not to be confused with Christmas. In some families, children manage to collect both.

Chutzpah—Latin derivative—audacity. In Anglo-Saxon means one hell of a nerve.

Gehachte leber—Chopped liver. Not bought at the delicatessen. Chopped in a wooden bowl, noisily.

Goyim—Gentiles, or like the way some Jews behave.

Kein ahurra—Wards off the evil eye. You don't have to hire an exorcist.

Machutunim (plural)—and *Machuteneste* (female, singular)—the family of the son-in-law or daughter-in-law. Mostly a hostile relationship, though sometimes concealed, not like the Capulets and Montagues. Big problem when it comes to decisions on wedding invitations.

Mishpucha—Relatives: good, bad, liked, unliked, rich, poor. And *their* in-laws, chosen and unchosen.

Mishugas—Craziness. Used for other people. For yourself, it's eccentricity. Loosely, a *mishugane* is one who disagrees with you.

Mitzvah—Blessing. Sometimes undisguised.

Momser—Literally bastard, but often used affectionately, having nothing to do with illegitimacy. Unless you mean it that way.

Olav hasholem—Requiescat in pace.

Pipick—Belly button. Known in some circles as a navel.

Potch—A slap. But much harder in Yiddish.

Schlump—A slob, not necessarily a fat one, but usually slow. A slow slob.

Sheitel—Wig worn by married, religious women, the purpose of which is to make them unattractive to other men. Now worn by the unmarried and irreligious. The purpose has been changed.

Shiksa—A Gentile girl, or a Jewish girl who might just as well be.

Sit *Shiva*—Week's mourning for the dead while everybody brings in food.

Tshatchkes—Any small ornament you don't know how to describe.

Tsuris—The cross you have to bear. Heavier in Yiddish and louder.

Tuchis—The part of you that you sit on. Used freely for spanking children and for off-color jokes and for saying where you'd like to kick someone.

Verdrehen mir ein kopf—Don't twist my head around.

Yarmulka—Skullcap worn by religious men. Covers bald spots.